ADAM BOUSE

# You Are Nature

*On Walking, Forest Bathing, and Coming Home to the Natural World*

OPTIMISTIC
COACHING

Cover design by Adam Bouse
Cover photograph "Forest Steps" by Adam Bouse
Original photograph available at unsplash.com/@adambouse
Book text set in Merriweather.

www.optimism.coach

First edition

ISBN: 979-8-9954779-0-7

This book was professionally typeset on Reedsy.
Find out more at reedsy.com

# Contents

# Acknowledgments

Brief excerpts from the following works are used under fair use for purposes of literary observation, commentary, and critique:

- "The Singular and Cheerful Life" from *Evidence* by Mary Oliver (Beacon Press, 2009)
- "Sometimes" from *Red Bird* by Mary Oliver (Beacon Press, 2008)
- "This Land Is Your Land" from *Dust Bowl Ballads* by Woody Guthrie (Ludlow Music, 1945)
- *A Psalm for the Wild-Built* by Becky Chambers (Tordotcom, 2021)
- *Braiding Sweetgrass* by Robin Wall Kimmerer (Milkweed Editions, 2013)

Grateful acknowledgment is made to the respective authors, estates, and publishers.

# Introduction

I wrote this book because I think we know, deep down, time outdoors is what we need. We've just forgotten how to do it.

We belong outside. You and I are *part of* nature.

There is a younger version of me who waded into a Kentucky creek as a kid, who lay in the grass in Yellowstone National Park listening to the forest with his eyes closed, who spent years plowing fields and tending a garden at a living history museum in Indiana.

There is also a version of me well-versed in the tech startup world, where productivity hacks and optimization were oxygen and grind culture was the weather.

Regardless of whether you experienced nature connection as a kid or found yourself very much addicted to screens as an adult, I'm here to tell you there is a path toward something more grounded and alive. And not metaphorically.

For me, it was literally through the woods, along rivers, across prairies, and eventually into a sunflower field at Conner Prairie where an eleven-year-old version of me showed up, uninvited, and invited forty-three-year-old me back into my place in nature.

That story is in these pages. So are the stories of seasons and trees and metaphors and a great-grandfather's Sunday walks. So is the science—what happens in our blood and our brains and our nervous systems when we slow down long enough to let nature do what it has always done.

This is a short book, and that's intentional. It comes in two parts. The first is personal—essays about my own winding experiences in nature and what I've found there. The second is practical—the science of why it works, the practice of forest bathing, and an invitation to build your own rhythm of being outdoors.

This isn't a new lifehack. I don't want to optimize your relationship with nature or give you another thing to measure.

I wrote it because something in me needed to say, as clearly and honestly as I could: we are not separate from the natural world. We are part of it. And remembering that—really letting it in—can change the way you breathe, the way you think, and the way you move through your life.

Let's see what's possible, you and me in nature.

# I

# PERSONAL ESSAYS

# From Kentucky to Yellowstone to the Prairie

*This land is your land, this land is my land*
*From California to the New York island,*
*From the redwood forest to the Gulf Stream waters;*
*This land was made for you and me.*
— Woody Guthrie

*I want to make certain that people connect with their 'cradle'*
*and recognize that natural landscapes are the nursery*
*for all human cultures worldwide.*
— Shelton Johnson

* * *

Many of my childhood summers included visits to my grandma's farm in rural central Kentucky.

We lived in suburban central Indiana, entirely average neighborhoods disconnected from my family's recent past in farming.

During those visits, I fished for crawdads in the "crick," with my pant legs rolled up, wading shin-deep into the chilly, fresh water. We wandered the rolling hills. I stared at the stars in an endless night sky. I jumped along the wall of hay bales lined up along the fence line, and learned all about snakes, chiggers, and ticks from my grandma.

One particular visit involved my grandma and me "fetching" a ground-hog that a neighbor had shot off a fence and offered to us. My grandpa skinned it and proceeded to turn it into our barbecued dinner that night.

We also stopped in at Mammoth Cave on a few of those Kentucky trips — both a national park and the world's largest surveyed cave system at 426 miles, more than double the second longest. The awe of standing in The Rotunda, a massive chamber 140 feet below the surface, is hard to compare to any above-ground experience. And with a slew of evocative chamber names — River Hall, Star Chamber, Giant's Coffin, Frozen Niagara, and Fat Man's Misery — you can understand how the wonder and imagination of a young child would be stoked to a roaring fire. Add in the fact that indigenous people explored and mined these caves for minerals as far back as 5,000 years ago, and it's easy to describe me as fascinated.

My visits to Kentucky planted something in me that has stayed throughout my life — seeds of longing to be out in nature, to be in awe at the scope, complexity, and mystery of it all.

Having unhurried time to walk in the woods, to sit by the ocean, or to notice the footprints of unseen animals along a riverbank — all of these experiences give me a sense of rootedness, with a heavy dose of feeling small, in the best way possible.

In addition to Kentucky, two other places shaped my love of nature during childhood: a living history museum in central Indiana and Yellowstone National Park.

* * *

A rite of passage for fourth graders in Indiana is a visit to Conner Prairie — a living history museum just outside of Indianapolis. Established by Eli Lilly (of pharmaceutical company fame) in the 1970s, the Conner Prairie of my childhood centered on life in Indiana between 1816 and

1836. Prairietown, a fictional composite town created to tell the story of life just after statehood, was constructed of buildings — some historic and moved to the site, others replicas. The town included a blacksmith shop, a carpenter, a potter, a doctor, and an inn, all staffed with fully costumed, well-studied "interpreters" there to play the part of 1830s-era Hoosiers and create interactive experiences for kids and families.

I distinctly remember the amazement I felt when a "gentleman farmer" took a break from chopping wood outside his single-room house to explain to me and a group of classmates how a sundial worked. The town had animals — oxen, chickens, pigs, and horses — along with hearths being tended by women cooking meals from scratch. No electricity, no running water. It was as if we had truly stepped back into 1836.

Conner Prairie became a formative experience in more ways than one. Not only did it deepen my connection to nature and the outdoors, it sparked a love of history that would eventually lead to a degree in history in college. And what was my first full-time job after graduation? Working at Conner Prairie for four years — plowing fields, milking cows, driving horses, slopping the hogs, tending the garden, and much more. I was a farmhand, a teacher, a balloon pilot, a snake oil salesman, and a historical interpreter.

* * *

A year after my fourth-grade trip to Conner Prairie, when I was eleven, my family took an epic two-week trip out West. In June of 1993, we packed everything into our van — fancy enough to have a separate cassette tape player in the back — along with a Sega Game Gear loaded with Sonic and a Game Boy with Dr. Mario and Teenage Mutant Ninja Turtles. We were regularly encouraged to put the screens down and notice what was just outside the windows.

We crossed over a swollen Mississippi River — the furthest west I had ever been, having grown up in central Indiana with only a trip or two to Chicago on my map. "The Great Flood of 1993" ended up costing $15 billion in damage, one of the most costly in U.S. history to that point. We made our way through Sioux City, Iowa and wandered through the Badlands on our way to Mount Rushmore.

Seeing the scope and scale of nature — first in the largest river in the country running well into flood stage, then in the barren, arid Badlands — I was already in awe before we reached the presidential faces carved into the mountain. We drove past Crazy Horse, the still-unfinished monument to the Lakota leader nearby, and my sense of how big the world was continued to expand.

Our furthest point west was Yellowstone National Park.

Hot springs, spouting geysers, waterfalls. We saw wild bison — an animal that appears on the seal of Indiana but had been driven out of the state around the same time my family was putting down roots in Kentucky, just before the Civil War. We saw a scorched forest from a wildfire the previous season. And at the Yellowstone Inn, I fulfilled the challenge that everyone in our family was held accountable to: you have to try at least one new food you've never had before. My dad and stepmom ordered bison burgers. I don't remember what my brothers had, but I fondly remember having blueberry cheesecake ice cream. I never felt closer to those who had ventured west to explore new lands.

Yellowstone is also where I made official my commitment to loving National Parks — which makes it sound like some kind of religious conversion, and maybe it was.

The National Park System has a program called Junior Park Rangers. Focused on education and awareness, kids check in at a park station, receive a program pamphlet from a ranger, and complete a series of activities and challenges to earn an official Junior Park Ranger badge.

Most of the activities were fairly straightforward — identify three types of trees, hike a trail, explore a visitor center. The most memorable, though, was a guided hike. I went on a group hike for kids with a ranger who took us about twenty minutes from the trailhead. He pointed out a few plant species and talked about the local ecosystem before asking us to find a comfortable spot to sit — or even lie down.

In his best Mr. Rogers voice, he explained that we can learn about a park not just through our eyes, but with our ears as well. We were to sit or lie with our eyes closed for five minutes, just listening to the world around us. I settled in and fought back a grin, chuckling because of the unusual sight, a group of eight- to twelve-year-olds sitting in silence with their eyes closed, just listening to nature.

When we opened our eyes, I noticed the pencil and blank sheet of paper in my lap. "Wait, what is this for?" I thought.

Our ranger instructed us to draw a map — not of the landscape or the trail, but of the sounds we'd heard during our silent time. "Create a map of the world around you that you can hear, even if you can't see it."

I created a swirling pattern of dashed lines to capture a flying bug — a bee or moth — I'd heard nearby. I scribbled a bumpy, scattered cloud of short, faint lines for the rustling leaves in the trees above. I drew a series of tiny, intertwining waterfalls to represent the bubbling creek that was just out of sight but unmistakable once I slowed down to pay attention.

This idea of sitting to listen to nature was entirely new to me, and it only deepened my admiration for it. I didn't have the words for it then, but I recognize that feeling now: awe, and a sense of connection to a larger story — the story of the sustained natural world all around me, one that doesn't need me to do anything for it to keep going, just as it has long before me and will long after.

* * *

I hadn't worked at Conner Prairie for fifteen years, but we had taken our kids many times, cycling in and out of annual memberships as I tried to give them the experiences I'd loved as a child, hoping they would love them too. Conner Prairie had expanded well beyond 1836 and now included a massive tethered helium balloon to explore the history of airmail in 1859 — I was actually a trained pilot for this before leaving in 2010, which I offer as a humble brag — and a Civil War area recounting the experience of families and soldiers during the 1860s.

In August of 2025, something new caught my attention. A notice for guided Forest Therapy sessions — offered twice a month in small groups, described as intentionally slow, relational, and gentle.

I registered for a Thursday afternoon session, eager to have three hours of protected time in a guided forest bathing experience. I had been reading up on the philosophy and practices and studying a professional coaching framework for nature-based work — taking traditional coaching clients into outdoor environments to unlock new mindsets, creativity, and possibilities.

It may not be surprising that even as my career as an executive, leadership, and management coach had thrived in recent years — working in a tech startup where optimization and grind culture were the default settings — I was still looking for ways to weave my long-held love of nature into my coaching philosophy and practice.

Still, I had never actually been part of a forest bathing session. I had only read about it.

On this unseasonably mild August day, it was just me and one other participant, Dheepa, along with our guide, Michelle. After brief introductions, we walked down to the edge of the floodplain — an open 200 acres nestled in a horseshoe bend of the White River. At an edge zone between woods and fields, we settled in for a short meditation to slow down and arrive. Michelle guided us through it, then invited us to share what had brought us to this experience and what intentions, if any, we were carrying into the session.

Next, Michelle explained that we would move through a series of invitations, each lasting fifteen or twenty minutes, to help us engage with our senses and the nature around us. Just down the hill from where we'd started was a sunflower field. We would begin by wandering down at our own pace and simply noticing movement — what was in motion, what was still, in whatever way we were aware of it. Dheepa and I smiled in delighted agreement and started down toward the field.

It was at that moment that something entirely unexpected happened. Like a wave crashing over me, I was suddenly flooded with the memory of lying on my back in Yellowstone National Park. I felt like my eleven-year-old self again. Even now it feels a little embarrassing to put into words. It was as if my inner child was fully present to my forty-three-year-old self — the two versions of me in a kind of silent conversation, seeing and acknowledging and welcoming each other.

My eyes welled up. A mixture of awe, wonder, astonishment, and contentment moved through me. I slowed to a near standstill, taking an occasional step as I smiled and shook my head in a kind of befuddled amazement, soaking in a transcendent feeling that lasted a few minutes.

I don't know if Dheepa or Michelle noticed anything unusual — in that moment or later on. We continued through a variety of invitations: smelling flowers, listening intently while cupping our ears, lying on our backs to observe the forest canopy, walking through the damp grass in our bare feet. For the next two and a half hours, it was peaceful. It was energizing. It was calming.

I loved every moment of the experience. I can't promise that anyone — or even I — should expect a transcendent moment like that one. But even without that deeply meaningful opening, the rest of the guided session was accessible, learnable, and genuinely supportive. It grounded me and gave me a sense of real connection — to myself and to nature.

I have since earned a certification in forest therapy and led my own sessions of forest bathing and nature-based coaching. Anyone can benefit from a self-led experience of simply, mindfully walking a trail, just as much as from a guided group experience in a forest, park, or wilderness area.

* * *

*What, in the earth world,*
   *is there not to be amazed by*
   *and to be steadied by*
   *and to cherish?*

From "The Singular and Cheerful Life," by Mary Oliver

# A Multitude of Metaphors



*The hopeful notion that new life is hidden in dying*
*is surely reinforced by the visual glories of autumn.*
— Parker Palmer

*Plants and animals will always amaze us.*
*Let's be amazed together.*
— Peter Wohlleben

* * *

A grounding exercise is a way to help an individual or a group slow down and be more present — in mind and body.

When I'm leading group coaching sessions with managers or leaders, they usually arrive straight from another meeting, already anticipating the next one, with a running list of urgent demands waiting on them. Those two to five minutes of grounding matter.

Sometimes I use the metaphor of having thirty tabs open in your browser — and we both know how good it feels to close a bunch of them, and how much better the remaining ones perform when you're not running twenty things at once.

"What I'd like you to do," I say, after talking about the tabs, "is take a piece of paper and pen — or do this on your computer — and make a running list of everything on your mind right now. What are all the tabs open in your thinking and feeling right now?"

I usually give them about ninety seconds. Rarely, if ever, does anyone come up empty.

"Next, I'd like you to simply slide that list out of reach. Put it in a drawer, close the notebook, or minimize the window. Consider this a physical invitation to let your brain release those things until our session is over. The list is there. It will be waiting for you. And by doing this, you're saying to your brain: I've written these things down, so you don't need to keep holding them. We'll pick them back up when we're done."

Many people have found this freeing and calming, and have told me so. Some, I imagine, have gone on to make it a practice they reach for anytime they want to be fully present to whoever or whatever is right in front of them.

## The Seasons

Recently, I've been opening group sessions with a different metaphor: the seasons. This exercise is an invitation to expand your awareness of where you are — in the world, in your story, in your experience.

Parker Palmer, in his essay "Seasons," writes about the particular usefulness of seasonal metaphors. This is the passage I read to open the exercise:

> *Most of us have a metaphor, conscious or not, that names our experience of life. Animated by the imagination — one of the most vital powers we possess — our metaphors are more than mirrors to reality. They often become reality, transmuting themselves from language into the living of our lives. Seasons is a wise metaphor for the movement of life, I think. It suggests that life is neither a battlefield nor a game of chance but something infinitely richer,*

*more promising, more real. The notion that our lives are like the eternal cycle of the seasons does not deny the struggle or the joy, the loss or the gain, the darkness or the light, but encourages us to embrace it all — and to find in all of it opportunities for growth.*

After about twenty seconds of silent reflection, I offer the group these prompts:

*What stands out to you? Any keywords or phrases? What res- onated? How does this metaphor point you toward something true?*

A leader I once worked for observed that every season has both a purpose and a struggle:

> **Spring** — planting and risk-taking
> **Summer** — playing and anticipating
> **Fall** — harvesting and closing out
> **Winter** — reflecting and pruning

We can't control the season we're in, but we can embrace it.

All seasons require work and rest, action and contemplation. We can't force the end of a particular season, though we can stay awake to the signs of transition. The wisdom, I've found, is in giving yourself permission to be in the season you're in — making the most of what that season asks of you, and letting go of the wish that things were otherwise.

Take a few minutes now to reflect.

*What season do you find yourself in? How accepting are you of that season? What joys and struggles would you like to name as present in this particular season for you? Who can you share* your reflections with?

## The Garden as Metaphor

Over the summer, I received a package from England I had been eager to hold in my hands.

I placed my order in May, knowing it would take a while to travel across the pond. When July came and it still hadn't arrived, I emailed to ask if perhaps it had gotten lost. Kindly, Ally responded with grace and generosity, saying she would send a replacement at no cost. By mid-August, I finally held it in my hands.

"Tending to Endings is a card deck for reimagining our relationship to endings," the website reads. It goes on: "We live in an era of escalating upheaval and crisis. To navigate these times we need to get better at 'hospicing' the systems, behaviors, and ideas that no longer work for us. Drawing on the garden as a metaphor, this deck helps us see endings as part of life's natural cycles. It offers imaginative yet grounded ways into difficult terrain, whether personal, collective, or systemic."

It is a beautiful, thoughtfully made deck — twelve cards in all, each one offering a metaphor from the garden, the farm, and the natural world.

*Composting. Coppicing. Deadheading. Fallowing. The Bonfire.*

Each card comes with an illustration, a few sentences describing the process, five additional words to broaden your vocabulary, and finally a few words of intention, invitation, and invocation to meditate on.

The deck is a powerful collection of metaphors — a beautiful offering for anyone in or anticipating an ending of any kind. A season. A job. A project. A relationship. A life.

I've brought these cards into coaching sessions, most notably a group session called "Putting the Season to Bed" in December. It was a kind of year-in-review, without the celebrations or the typical stats. "A quiet inventory of your year. Feel the release of a hearty exhale through guided reflections and group conversation" — that was how I described it.

The cards offer a nature-based language and wisdom — another portal into seeing the cycles of life as natural, present, and generative.

* * *

*Loss and renewal is the perennial, eternal, transformative pattern. It's like a secret spiral: each time you allow the surrender, each time you can trust the dying, you will experience a new quality of life within you.*
— *Richard Rohr*

## The Universal Pattern

I've written elsewhere about what I call the Universal Pattern — order, disorder, reorder — and how everything in nature and the universe seems to follow it.

Order — Disorder — Reorder
Life — Death — Rebirth
Construction — Deconstruction — Reconstruction

I have a tattoo that reflects this: two overlapping circles with short lines radiating from one side. It reminds me every day to find acceptance in whatever part of the cycle I find myself in.

Visually, my tattoo can be simply that — a geometric pattern. But it also represents a sunrise or a sunset, a solar eclipse beginning or ending, roots going deep and sprouts shooting up. It's the pattern of our seasons, of how plants grow and thrive, and it is woven throughout our lives and relationships for those who have eyes to see it.

When we know and name our endings — in metaphor or otherwise — we can have a relationship with them rather than resisting or denying them. Moving through an ending may feel like a complete undoing. And yet, as Parker Palmer reminds us, there is a hopeful notion that new life is hidden in dying.

Tending to our endings is how we make space for what comes next. It's part of the cycle. Everything belongs.

## These Things Happen

I've been sitting with a phrase lately that is changing how I see daily life. "These things happen."

The disappointments, the interruptions, the confusion, the mistakes, the letdowns. And also — the joy, the delights, the laughter, the pleasant surprises.

A project gets derailed. A meeting goes south. A kid doesn't want to do chores. A drink spills. A gathering gets canceled. Another driver backs into your parked car. The heavy sighs roll in, the resentment builds, and the mental state begins to slink.

"These things happen" is a way to practice acceptance.

I could try resisting reality — pushing back on things I wish weren't true, as if my resistance could undo the trajectory of things I never had control over in the first place. If you're like me, you can spend a lot of energy wishing for something different, spinning up arguments about why it isn't fair, it's bad timing, it's not what was supposed to happen.

But "these things happen" reminds me that disappointments, interruptions, confusion, mistakes, and letdowns do, in fact, happen. When I see them as part of the normal texture of experience — something to be expected at a certain level, part of the story rather than an interruption of it — I'm living in a whole new way.

From this place of acceptance, I maintain my ability to choose how I engage with challenges — rather than spinning out of control or falling into frustration, entitlement, or disgust. In fits and starts, I'm trying to remember: these things happen.

This is not the same as accepting injustice, abuse, marginalization, exclusion, or hate. Those things must be named, engaged with, and actively worked against — to make "what could be" real. But to act as if we live in a world where those things simply don't exist would be its own form of denial.

In the end, accepting doesn't mean giving up or giving in. It means seeing clearly.

(This is the beginning of what I call "grounded optimism" — something I write about elsewhere and have devoted much of my professional work toward cultivating.)


## Two Parables

### *Maybe, Maybe Not*

A farmer and his son had a beloved horse who helped the family earn a living. One day, the horse ran away and their neighbors exclaimed, "Your horse ran away — what terrible luck!" The farmer replied, "Maybe, maybe not."

A few days later, the horse returned, leading several wild horses back to the farm. The neighbors shouted, "Your horse has returned and brought others with him — what great luck!" The farmer replied, "Maybe, maybe not."

Later that week, the farmer's son was trying to ride one of the new horses and was thrown to the ground, breaking his leg. The neighbors cried, "Your son broke his leg — what terrible luck!" The farmer replied, "Maybe, maybe not."

A few weeks later, soldiers marched through town recruiting all able-bodied young men for the army. They did not take the farmer's son, because of his broken leg. The neighbors shouted, "Your boy is spared —

what tremendous luck!" To which the farmer replied, "Maybe, maybe not."

## An Alien's First Visit to Earth

An interstellar traveler arrived on Earth one September. At first, the being noticed the predominance of full, green, leafy trees all around the planet.

Come October, the leaves began to change — slowly at first, then in rapid succession, erupting into brilliant hues of red, yellow, and orange. By November, the leaves on most trees had lost their vibrancy, turned dull, and fallen to the ground.

Billions of trees. Trillions of dropped leaves. The trees standing silently, stark and barren. Any sense of aliveness seemingly stripped away.

In just three months, our space traveler has gone from appreciation to awe, from awe to concern, and from concern to sadness.

"Are they dying? What's wrong with the trees? Is it a disease? Why is this happening? Can you get them back? How do you stop it?"

Patiently, you respond: "This is the cycle — a universal cycle, in fact. Life, death, and then rebirth. I wonder what you've seen or experienced in your corner of the universe that follows the same flow.

"What you see here, now, is just a part of this cycle — not the end. It looks as though the trees have lost all their vitality. But this is actually the wisest thing they could do. They've shed what would become a burden through the windy, snowy months ahead. And they've shed only what they can recreate — re-create, to literally create again. They will regrow their leaves in due time, in the right season, and continue on in a brilliant cycle of life."

Why do the leaves fall?

These things happen.

They aren't a distraction from the story.
They are the story itself.

# I Think About Being a Tree

*Learn character from trees, values from roots, and change from leaves.*
— Tasneem Hameed

*We are called to assist the Earth, to heal her wounds and in the process heal our own — indeed, to embrace the whole creation in all its diversity, beauty, and wonder.*
— Wangari Maathai

* * *

Anyone who knows me, even a little, knows Fall is my favorite time of year.

I have my fall playlist — lots of folk, acoustic, and bluegrass. My checklist of seasonal movies: *Dan in Real Life, When Harry Met Sally, The Village.* Recipes I dust off every year: apple butter, apple pie, pumpkin chocolate chip muffins. And plans to get out on trails around the state.

This is also when most people pay attention to trees — their brilliant displays ahead of entering dormancy for the long winter months. One full burst of color before the winter grey arrives.

And while I am captivated by and spend an inordinate amount of time photographing and oversharing photos of October and November foliage, I'm fascinated by trees all year round.

In addition to enjoying their beauty, their shade, and their fruit, I've come to think of trees as a meaningful way to think about living a life.

* * *

Perhaps it's common in your twenties and thirties to believe that life is really about applying what you know to be true — the principles, the insights, the wisdom. That if you do it right, things will go "up and to the right." Learn the principles, apply the principles, achieve the good life. Chart the progress. Measure the success.

Entering my forties — through hard experiences, anxiety and depression, job changes, a shifting relationship with my sense of spirituality and faith — the folly of that logic was laid bare. Life is not a chart. It cannot be distilled into a series of inputs and outputs.

If you look at life as a series of charts, always expecting to go "up and to the right," where can you end up other than exhausted and perpetually comparing yourself to what else could have been? It becomes easy to wonder why you're not making more progress, or whether you've fallen short of your "potential."

I'd rather think about being like a tree than optimizing the charts of my life.

I want to be rooted but flexible.

I want to provide cover and comfort to others.

I want to live in a symbiotic relationship with my environment.

I want to experience seasons of fruitfulness, along with seasons of rest.

I want longevity, perseverance, and resilience.

* * *

Over the last few years, we planted four trees around our house: two sycamores, one tulip poplar — the state tree of Indiana — and a Honeycrisp apple tree.

Sycamore trees take twenty-five years to reach maturity, with peak seed production happening somewhere between fifty and two hundred years of age. I didn't plant them for their seeds. But knowing that has opened my eyes to an entirely different timescale than I'm used to considering.

(It also occurred to me that there are no bad trees. They are all good trees. It's only when we impose our expectations or needs onto them that their goodness gets thwarted. Whatever they look like, however they grow, they are simply full of treeness — being exactly what they are supposed to be.)

* * *

In modern life, our timescale is tied to instant "read" receipts on text messages, Google searches that predict and autocomplete our typing, and same-day shipping with constant tracking. A few years ago, I was stunned to receive an email from the United States Postal Service that included a photoscan of every piece of mail being delivered to my mailbox that day. My only thought was: how is this even a thing?

Everything is increasingly designed around urgency, immediacy, and efficiency. Everything seems knowable, controllable, within reach.

But everything isn't knowable and controllable. Not really. And I think that's a good thing.

We need more mystery in our modern lives.

That's not a call to shut down science or knowledge. I love the way Father Richard Rohr describes mystery: "Mystery is not something you can't know. Mystery is endless knowability."

This moves us beyond a kind of finite, data-driven knowing into something more mystical, curious, and open-handed. Knowing of many kinds.

So I ask myself: How might I resist the temptation to make everything knowable and controllable? What does it look like to be patient enough to wait for fruit and seeds — in the right season, or the right decade — to show up in my life? How might I practice being satisfied in simply being, rather than producing or optimizing?

Where are expectations and needs thwarting my own goodness — my own kind of treeness?

All of this requires more sitting with, more wondering. It is an invitation to embrace mystery.

## Houseplants with Complicated Emotions

Last year, I only grew tomatoes in a raised bed. This year I overdid it.

Tomatoes, green and banana peppers, cucumbers, green beans, cantaloupe, and blueberries. Each with varying needs and requirements — which is why I've likely spread myself too thin. Trying to be good at growing all of them means I'm not succeeding at helping any of them thrive. So I fall back on what I know.

Here's what I know: Seeds and soil. Sunlight and darkness. Weed, wait, and harvest. There aren't many other ways to grow something. This is true for plants, too.

On a personal level — creatively and mentally — I find myself somewhere between the sunlight and the darkness. In a season of relative dormancy, wanting more but not finding the inner energy to go beyond what each day requires, one day at a time.

It's tempting to resist — to push and force myself into solving more problems, producing more ideas, contributing to more things. To go from growing tomatoes to growing the entire produce section, metaphorically speaking.

But with age I've begun, finally, to learn the wisdom of seasons: no person can constantly produce, constantly be in growth mode. Humans need time for dormancy, for maintenance, for rest. Rest can still be active — but it's different from breaking new ground.

One of my favorite lines I've come across: "Literally nothing in the universe operates at 100%... one hundred percent of the time."

In a recent group coaching session on rest and recovery, I used this illustration to open a conversation:

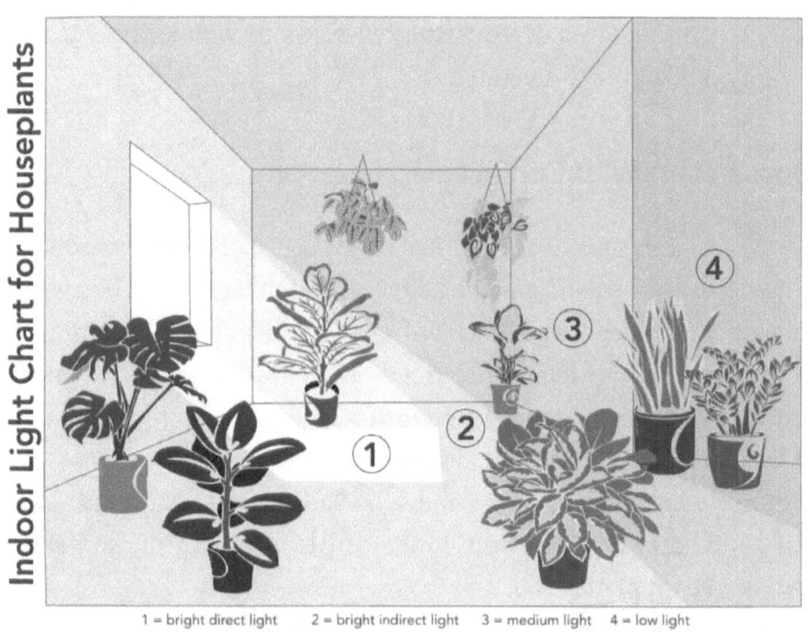


*Indoor Light Chart for Houseplants. (n.d.). [Graphic]. Succulents Box.*
*https://succulentsbox.com*

Not every plant thrives in full sunlight — others won't survive without it. But every plant needs periods of darkness and rest. More than sixteen hours of sunlight and virtually all plants lose their ability to photosynthesize — the process by which they convert sunlight into energy. Too much of a good thing is, in fact, bad for a plant. Darkness and rest are part of a healthy lifecycle.

And we all know humans are essentially houseplants with complicated emotions.

We need good soil, sunlight, water — and the rest. (This is true both as metaphor and in quite literal ways, as we'll explore soon enough.)

So how do you prioritize what may not come naturally — rest and recovery? Where are you overexposed, in need of shade, or the quiet dark of a night to simply rest in?

Those complicated emotions get even more complicated when we aren't meeting our physical and mental needs.

Plant and water. Sunlight and darkness. Weed, wait, and harvest.

There aren't many other ways to grow.

This is true for people, too.

# It Takes 20 Minutes to Walk a 20-Minute Mile

*In my afternoon walk I would fain forget all my morning occupations and
my obligations to Society. But it sometimes happens that I cannot easily
shake off the village. The thought of some work will run in my head and I
am not where my body is — I am out of my senses. In my walks I would fain
return to my senses. What business have I in the woods,
if I am thinking of something out of the woods?*
— Henry David Thoreau

* * *

I decided to take a walk.

I try to do this most days now — to keep my body in motion, to clear my mind, to get out of the house. Since I work from home, that last one matters more than it might sound.

If I walk the outside loop of my neighborhood, it's just short of an even mile. Some days I use it for meditation or mindfulness. Other times I'll listen to a podcast. And occasionally, I let my brain wander wherever it wants to go.

One day, I picked an audiobook I was trying to finish before the library loan expired. My mind was drifting, switching between things I needed to get done and the words coming through my earbuds.

Somewhere around fifteen minutes in, my brain snapped back to full awareness of the present moment. And I thought: Why am I still walking? Why am I not back home yet? A flicker of impatience colored my mind.

And then, from somewhere deeper, a response arose:
*Because it takes 20 minutes to take a 20-minute walk.*

I set out to go for a mile walk.
Not a mile run.
Not to check something off my list.
Not to be able to say I went on a walk.

I found myself almost chuckling at the realization that I had wanted to more efficiently get done with a walk. It sounds ridiculous, even reading it back to myself now.

Things take the time they take.

I could have pumped my elbows, lengthened my stride, raised my heart rate — until the walk was no longer a walk. It would have become a jog. Or a run. Those aren't bad things; I do them on occasion. But the moment you change something, it ceases to be the thing it was.

It left me wondering: what other 20-minute walks am I trying to just get through — inflicting the violence of efficiency or optimization on them, changing their very nature?

I'm on the lookout.

* * *

An article from 2019, "We're Optimizing Ourselves to Death," came to mind later that day. It named something I'd been circling:

> *The acceleration of our collective pace of life is not a result of stupidity or irrationality; rather, it is a symptom of what is perfectly predicted by the prisoner's dilemma at a global scale: hyperrational individuals making hyperrational decisions on how to spend their time by launching into an inescapable arms race of productivity. Burnout is inevitable. We're playing a rigged game, and every time we do, our pace of life accelerates, and the world moves faster.*

And this:

> *Attempts by companies like Google or Freshly to create services that save you time misfire, as millennials see them not as services that will give them more time to relax, but as services that will increase the amount of time they're available to work.*

I recognized myself in that second quote — and not just because I'm a geriatric millennial. That flicker of "Why am I not done with this walk yet?" was the arms race showing up in my own neighborhood loop.

* * *

Some things aren't meant to be optimized, only experienced. Some things shouldn't be hacked, only brought into unhurried presence. And still other things could be hacked, but we'd be wise to resist the temptation. As the saying goes: we realized we could, but never stopped to ask whether we should.

I wonder: what would you put on the list of things that deserve to be experienced unencumbered by efficiency, maximization, and productivity?

* * *

Maybe the summer lulls me into a more slumberous existence — causing me to slow my pace, temper my efforts.  I say this thinking very specifically of a Kurt Vonnegut interview:

*"Oh, she says, well, you're not a poor man. You know, why don't you go online and buy a hundred envelopes and put them in the closet?" And so I pretend not to hear her.  And go out to get an envelope because I'm going to have a hell of a good time in the process of buying one envelope.  I meet a lot of people.  And see some great-looking babes. And a fire engine goes by. And I give them the thumbs up. And ask a woman what kind of dog that is. And, I don't know.*

*The moral of the story is, we're here on Earth to fart around. And of course the computers will do us out of that. And what the computer people don't realize, or they don't care, is we're dancing animals. You know, we love to move around.  And we're not supposed to dance at all anymore.*

I think I'll go take another 20-minute walk now.

# Walk Your Problems

*"Keep walking, though there's no place to get to."*
— Rumi

* * *

In my mid-20s, I remember my grandma telling me stories about her childhood in rural Kentucky, and her dad Louis Weston.

She showed me this family photo [pictured below]—her mom, dad, the first of her two younger brothers, and herself—taken around 1937 or 1938.  She couldn't recall the exact reason they were taking a family photo, but she did recall "Daddy hit his head on a piece of machinery in the barn," explaining the white bandage wrapped around his head.

*My great-grandfather, Louis Weston, with his family (c. 1937)*

Born and raised in Kentucky, he was a farmer first. Eventually, he would also open a country general store. But one thing he was consistent about,

Grandma would tell me, was his Sunday walks. Every Sunday afternoon, after church and "dinner" (lunch), Louis would head off on his own for a Sunday walk.

There's no record of what he was thinking about, where exactly he went, or how far he went. Still, you can imagine he was thinking about the week just past and anticipating the coming one. Maybe he was allowing his mind to wander to other interests or news he had heard from folks at the general store. He could have been in prayer or simply enjoying time to have nothing in particular to accomplish, aside from putting one foot in front of the other. I imagine he saw critters, skipped stones on the creek, and maybe even "called on" a few neighbors he hadn't heard from in some time.

When I heard about his Sunday walks—I loved the idea. A ritual and rhythm of simply getting outdoors, no agenda or expectations. Walking, not in a hurry, and having a predictable practice of walking.

* * *

Søren Kierkegaard, writing to his sister-in-law who struggled with both depression and physical ailments, offered this advice:

> *Above all, do not lose your desire to walk: every day I walk myself into a state of well-being and walk away from every illness; I have walked myself into my best thoughts, and I know of no thought so burdensome that one cannot walk away from it... but by sitting still, and the more one sits still, the closer one comes to feeling ill... Thus if one just keeps on walking, everything will be all right.*

* * *

Two of my own literary heroes, C.S. Lewis and J.R.R. Tolkien, practiced the art of walking as well.

> *"Walking and talking are two very great pleasures, but it is a mistake to combine them. Our own noise blots out the sounds and silences of the outdoor world; and talking leads almost inevitably to smoking, and then farewell to nature as far as one of our senses is concerned. The only friend to walk with is one who so exactly shares your taste for each mood of the countryside that a glance, a halt, or at most a nudge, is enough to assure us that the pleasure is shared."* — C.S. Lewis

Tolkien's most famous line about walking comes from his beloved work, *The Lord of the Rings*:

*"Not all who wander are lost."*

While I don't think Lewis or I would want to exclusively separate walking from meaningful conversation, it still holds that the right *kind* of conversation or intention when heading out on a trail or down by the river can unlock a kind of experience you won't find by *mindlessly* conversing or heading out for solitude in nature.

There is much wisdom in walking. For obvious health reasons, in our modern, sedentary lives, of course—but also because of the way it shifts our thinking and our way of being.

Even a simple 15–20 minute walk can unlock new levels of energy, creativity, and mental clarity.

* * *

Manoush Zomorodi is a journalist, podcast host, and author of three books:

- *Bored and Brilliant: How Spacing Out Can Unlock Your Most Productive and Creative Self* (2017)
- *Spark: How to Free Your Brain From Technology to Ignite Your Creativity* (2020)
- *Body Electric: The Hidden Costs of the Digital Age and the New Science to Reclaim Your Well-Being* (2026)

Through her podcast and books, she has become a consistent and compelling advocate for average, everyday movement. Her writing regularly unpacks research and points to sustainable ways to move your body and reap the benefits.

Simple walks—even just five to thirty minutes—can help counteract the effects of too much sitting and too much screen time. Zomorodi unpacks the research clearly:

- **Improved metabolic and heart health:** short, regular walks lower blood pressure and reduce glucose levels
- **Mental boosts:** higher productivity, better focus, and lower fatigue
- **Creativity boosts:** the brain's default mode network (DMN) allows for mind wandering that contributes to imagination, creativity, and novel ideas
- **Long-term improvements:** research indicates daily walking may reduce the risk of chronic diseases, including Alzheimer's and various cancers

* * *

You know how beneficial it is to be in a space where you aren't hyper-focused, a place where your mind can wander while you almost mindlessly move through a particular activity. I'm talking about the shower.

Whether it's going for a stroll, taking a shower, or sitting on an airplane—these loosely engaged states of mind let us soften our executive brain's fixation on a problem or opportunity. And when that happens, the problem or opportunity gets tossed around in other parts of the brain, below the surface of direct awareness, until all of a sudden we have a new idea, a breakthrough, or a revelation.

Sometimes, when you're looking directly at a puzzle, it's impossible to see the solution. Only when we step away, create space, and allow other ways of knowing to enter our mental, emotional, and spiritual conversation can we find the path we are looking for.

This was the inspiration for a leadership workshop I led in October of 2025. "Walk Your Problems: A Nature-based Workshop for Optimism and Resilience." The idea was simple: bring a small group outdoors and allow nature to be co-coach, allowing participants to find renewed optimism, resilience, and creativity from and because of being in nature.

Ten participants joined me at Munsee Woods, a former Girl Scout camp now being restored into a nature preserve by the people at Red-tail Conservancy, for a three-hour nature-based experience.

We started with introductions—sharing why we were all interested in this particular experience (spoiler: everyone there loves time in nature) and some grounding ideas around the concepts of optimism and resilience. We did a breathing exercise, waited a few minutes for a downpour to pass, and then into the woods we went!

Through several guided exercises, we reconnected with nature...and ourselves. People reflected that they felt more relaxed, at ease, and able to focus on the experience without being distracted by their phones.

And that's what the experience was about—slowing down to intentionally be part of nature, not just in it or near it. Allowing nature to be a partner, a contributor to your well-being. Letting it coach you on ways of being.

Early on, I asked the participants to think of a current challenge or problem they were facing. Something that was important to them but isn't yet resolved. And then I told them to let it go to the back of their mind, to set it aside and not worry about thinking about the problem anymore.

This is another benefit of time in nature, or even just taking a walk through your neighborhood: it gives your consciously aware, problem-solving executive brain a chance to shift out of solving, sorting, and deciding.

The concept of "soft fascination" has been studied in recent years as a way of "attending to softly fascinating stimuli" that "not only requires little effort but also leaves mental space for reflection." (We will talk more in depth about this in Section II.) Background processing in the brain—the kind that happens below conscious awareness—gets more room during these moments. That may be why you have "aha!" moments in the shower, feel more creative when traveling, or find fresh ideas while hiking through a forest or near a large body of water.

* * *

I can't promise that walking your problems will make all your challenges melt away. No one told me on that day that they had experienced a massive breakthrough or had a million-dollar idea. But what they did communicate was that they felt calmer, their shoulders had dropped, and though it took a little while to settle in, the constant churn of tasks and reminders and anticipation that normally sits at the forefront of their attention...got quieter.

Imagine if you were able to find a rhythm of walks in which you experienced something quieter, softer, gentler. Imagine having a predictable way of tapping into creativity, optimism, and fresh thinking.

Maybe it's time to take a walk and see what's possible.

* * *

# INTERLUDE

*A pause, before we continue.*

If you've made it this far, you've been walking with me for a while—through Kentucky and Yellowstone, through seasons and parables, through a sunflower field where time seemed to fold in on itself. Thank you for coming this far. I'm grateful.

Now for a shift.

The first half of this book was personal essays, reflections. I told you these stories because they reflect what I've experienced and because they're the truest way I know to say what I mean. I can talk about the science of nature all day, but the truth is, I didn't come to love the woods because of a research paper. I love them because of a creek in Kentucky, a ranger in Yellowstone, a moment in a field that I still can't fully explain—and a thousand other untold, small, quiet moments.

The second half of this book is where I zoom out, just a little bit. In the chapters ahead, we'll look at what science has discovered about why nature does what it does to us: to our attention, our stress, our immune systems, our sense of self. We'll explore the practice of forest bathing. And we'll talk about what it looks like to build a life with more sky, trees, water, and soil in it.

The science matters. It's real and it's compelling. But if I had to choose between knowing why a walk in the woods lowers my cortisol and simply taking the walk—I'd take the walk every time.

I hope you will too.

# II

# THE SCIENCE AND THE PRACTICE OF NATURE

# There is a World Beyond the Screens

*Instead of asking, "Have I worked hard enough to rest?" I've started asking, "Have I rested enough to do my most meaningful work?"*
— Dana McGowan

*"I have met with but one or two persons in the course of my life who understood the art of Walking, that is, of taking walks—who had a genius, so to speak, for SAUNTERING..."*
— Henry David Thoreau

* * *

When someone asks me why I enjoy spending time in nature, especially walking in the woods, my response typically begins with: *"Because I'm surrounded by something larger than myself and I'm not responsible for any of it."*

Even in the relatively modest forests and state parks of Indiana, the feeling of being both small and connected is real. I hope, someday soon, to stand next to the giant redwoods and sequoias on the West Coast, their size and scope dwarfing anything I could find in Indiana.

I don't need to be in a dense forest, though. When I'm out in a park, a wide field, or along a river, something deep in me feels at home—amidst the deep greens high and low, in the breeze filtering through the trees, in the uneven footing of the field, and in the wetness of the soil along a riverbank.

There is a regular feeling of awe, if I slow down enough to notice it.

Here is this entire ecosystem that requires nothing of me in order to operate and maintain itself—nothing, that is, except not corrupting or destroying it. I didn't make the forest, nor do I actively maintain it or contribute to its essential components. It's both freeing and contrary to so many other aspects of my life, where I'm responsible for paying bills, cooking food, doing laundry, repairs around the house, dusting shelves, vacuuming carpets, taking cars in for maintenance, and so much more.

Spending time in nature is the best kind of selfish for me—I thoroughly enjoy it and am replenished by it, and it asks so little of me. When I think of rest and recovery, time in nature is what I know to be most effective.

## Biophilia and Soft Fascination

*Biophilia* is a scientific hypothesis suggesting that humans possess an innate, instinctive, evolutionary desire to be connected to the natural world. This matches my experience, but I fully understand if that sense isn't immediately discernible for everyone.

Imagine growing up in a dense urban environment. Instead of a green canopy, crunchy leaves, the scent of earth, and the sound of endless creatures—you experienced the "concrete jungle." Constant noise from people, cars, machines, and the echo of it all bouncing off steel skyscrapers.

You wouldn't need to grow up in or live in the middle of Times Square to experience this, either—even light urban or suburban environments today are filled with noise, both environmental and individually created. Headphones and earbuds have become constant companions for many people as they walk to work, walk their dog, or walk to the end of the driveway to take out the trash. The endless stream of podcasts, music,

TV, and movies gives us plenty of reasons to create environments that block out the natural sounds all around us.

Sights and sounds are the easiest to compare between modern cityscapes and natural environments like a forest, prairie, or riverbank. But obviously the smells and physical sensations in these two very different environments create vastly different experiences.

And anytime you become accustomed to a particular environment—how it looks, feels, sounds, smells, and even tastes—any kind of change is going to, at first, have the potential to feel confusing, disorienting, uncomfortable, or even dangerous.

Go either direction on this spectrum—wilderness to the city, city to the wilderness—and you're likely to show a similar response of uncertainty, tentativeness, and maybe even fear. We tend to fear what we don't know, us humans, and that isn't just about fearing other people—it's also about our environment. Still, it's worth considering what getting back into nature can provide you that a city or neighborhood simply cannot, no matter how well designed.

Nature's ability to provide an environment that restores our mental resources is well documented, and in this and the following chapter, we'll explore what science has discovered along those lines. Attention, memory, energy, and creativity are just a few aspects of our mental and emotional reality that benefit from time in nature.

* * *

*Attention Restoration Theory* (ART) is one way to explain what's happening when we walk into the woods or hit the trail at a local or state park. First, though, we have to understand what we're giving our attention to—what is depleting our focus and concentration—and then consider how best to restore our attention reservoirs.

As the writer Annie Dillard famously observed, "How we spend our days is, of course, how we spend our lives." Multitasking, for some, is seen as a superpower for driving productivity. Answering emails while sitting in a meeting. Updating your calendar while talking to a coworker. Making dinner while listening to a podcast. Driving and texting.

Research shows that no one is truly capable of multitasking. What looks like doing several things at once is really constant task switching—and the more varied the tasks, the more taxing and error-prone the switching becomes. Most importantly—and hilariously—people who rate themselves highest on multitasking regularly rank lowest on actual performance. If you think you're good at it, you're probably worse at it than most.

The most recent upgrade to task switching is "continuous partial attention"—a term coined by former Apple and Microsoft executive Linda Stone. It describes the behavior of continuously scanning every information stream, especially digital ones, to make sure you're always "on," at least partially, so you don't miss anything. We stay in the shallow end of the engagement pool, skimming the surface and feeling more productive—but it raises stress, scatters our focus, and can even affect our breathing. The term "screen apnea" describes what happens when we prioritize the constant scan over deep, relaxed breathing and presence.

Let the words of writer Amy Krouse Rosenthal be a welcome warning: "PAY ATTENTION TO WHAT YOU PAY ATTENTION TO. That's pretty much all the info u need."

* * *

Let's say you give up the notion of multitasking. You're going to monotask. Close the laptop, shut off all the phone notifications, pull the office door closed. You focus for an hour, maybe two, on polishing the presentation you're working on—building slides, prepping your talk notes, rehearsing some of the delivery. You've successfully focused and concentrated and done great work.

You will *still* experience mental drain and eventually exhaustion, right? The question is: how do we build that back up? Because even in the best of circumstances, you have more decisions to make today, another important meeting to go to, kids to help with homework, a partner to connect with and hear about their day...and so on.

Psychologists have a term to describe our internal capacity to evaluate how our actions will contribute to positive outcomes in the future. They call it "psychological capital," or PsyCap.

PsyCap is composed of distinct components: hope, self-efficacy, resilience, and optimism. These factors contribute to our motivation and engagement with life, giving us the psychological capital to hold certain beliefs and take certain actions that turn into positive outcomes throughout our days and weeks.

Like any valuable resource, they can get depleted. When we focus and concentrate, there is both a physiological and psychological draw on our resources. So we need to build those resources back up—like taking money out of a bank account and then depositing your next paycheck.

This is where Attention Restoration Theory comes in. The theory, developed by environmental psychologists Rachel and Stephen Kaplan in 1995, proposes that restoration happens when four conditions come together: you get away from your everyday stresses, you're in an expansive space, you're doing something that fits your natural inclinations, and—crucially—you encounter stimuli that are "softly fascinating." When those conditions are met, the effortless, involuntary attention that nature invites allows your depleted, directed attention to recover.

In plain terms: get away from your routine, go somewhere that feels expansive, do something you actually want to do, and let your attention land softly on whatever catches it. Nature checks every one of those boxes.

Nature is not only enjoyable but can also help us restore and improve our focus and ability to concentrate. Instead of top-down focus and attention—cognitively draining—bottom-up awareness and recovery takes priority. Mind wandering, daydreaming, and divergent thinking can not only feel energizing but lead to more creativity and increased optimism.

Two key terms when exploring ART further: "effortless attention" and "soft fascination." Soft fascination is an antidote to focused concentration. Instead of task-driven, detail-oriented focus, soft fascination moves the brain into a different mode—one that is aware of your environment and surroundings but in a more effortless, restorative way. Research also shows a significant improvement in working memory performance, in addition to focus and concentration, following nature exposure. That makes sense, given that part of focusing and concentrating involves pulling in relevant context from our memory as we hold a conversation, work on a problem, or move toward an interesting opportunity.

With effortless attention, it's not that you're mindlessly existing as you sit beneath a cluster of trees or walk down a dirt path to a pond—it's that there is a more gentle, non-demanding way of being that doesn't require your mind to constantly evaluate, assess, and determine things with your executive brain. Your mind can actually rest while it remains engaged in a more contented way. Your senses are still taking in information and creating a certain relaxed mood, but noticing the variety of green shades in a single tree or observing a bee floating near a flower with curiosity isn't the same as trying to solve a budget problem or tracking the logistics of an upcoming trip.

You don't have to head off to a national park to experience soft fascination or effortless attention. Listening to nature sounds mindfully—a trickling stream, birdsong, rustling leaves—can create soft fascination if you bring it to the forefront, rather than letting it become just the soundtrack for your productivity session. Still, you can understand why being out in nature is more impactful than listening to Spotify or looking at a photo of wildflowers on your phone.

Nature exposure is accessible to almost all of us in one way or another, allowing the qualities of nature to attend to us and help us find restoration. Observing the colors of foliage, watching the play of light through trees, noticing patterns and textures in tiny insects, and the overall peaceful, unchallenging environment—all of it provides visual and sensory stimulation.

Studies have shown people relax most while seeing greens and blues. Think tree canopies, or a clear sky reflecting on a lake. And while a photo on your computer background isn't the same as being in a green space, research suggests that even a blue-and-green image of nature can be a microdose of soft fascination—and therefore, restoration.

What's also true is that we can show up in natural spaces and not be fully there—not mentally, not emotionally.

You can still benefit, in unseen and unfelt ways. But why waste the opportunity to slow down and engage with a different pace, a different way of breathing and seeing and being?

When a 20-minute walk in the park becomes something you find pleasure in, time can seem to warp—standing still or flying by. By being immersed in the moment, everything outside your present focus can get blurry. By being present, you begin to align your mental, emotional, and spiritual reality—which is another way of saying you are experiencing restoration, grounding, and satisfaction through soft fascination. It doesn't become a "fix" for the challenges or change the opportunities you might have been thinking about when you got out of your car at the trailhead parking lot, or when you walked down the street from your office to a city park—but it can change *you* and how you show up when you step back into the experience of your whole life.

* * *

Throughout this book are scattered different practices, tools, and invitations for how to engage mindfully when you are in nature.

There are endless "right ways" to practice, with only a few "wrong ways." Saying a way is *wrong* may seem a bit strong, but to experience the fullness of being mindfully in nature or forest bathing (as we'll discuss soon), I've found a few things that will undercut your best intentions:

• Listening to music, podcasts, audiobooks, or talking on the phone/-FaceTime

• Checking your phone for messages or notifications, or your smart-watch or other device for performance stats (heart rate, step count, calorie burn, etc.)

• Even checking your phone for the time can pull you out of a mindful experience—set a timer or alarm and trust it to bring you back when you need to finish or head back

• If you're with other people, be mindful of how much time you spend talking or sharing. While it can be valuable to be in nature with others, we can unintentionally reactivate our thinking-solving-evaluating brain and limit our ability to enter soft fascination and tap into the full sensory experience. Consider saving thoughts, observations, or sharing until a set time—such as an agreed-upon stopping point or check-in opportunity.

*In essence, the invitation is as simple as: "Be where your feet are."*

## A Secure Relationship with Nature

One of the more surprising findings I've come across while studying the impact of nature on humans is the role of attachment and secure relationships.

I'm not a therapist or psychologist (though I do have training in emotional intelligence and a certification in brain-based coaching), so understand that I'm synthesizing what I've learned from experts in those fields. I welcome corrections or a more nuanced understanding if you have one.

*Attachment Theory* is the idea that the way our primary caregivers responded to us as babies creates a "blueprint" for how we handle intimacy and trust as adults. If you felt safe and seen back then, you likely move through the world with a secure sense of connection; if not, you might find yourself constantly chasing reassurance or reflexively pushing people away to protect yourself. It's essentially an attempt to explain how our earliest bonds teach us whether the world is a reliable place to land or a minefield we have to navigate alone.

From my understanding, for example, you could have an anxious attachment style in your first few decades, but through your own inner work, therapy, and intentional practice, it is possible to develop a more secure style.

Here is where nature comes into play. Along with my surprise.

In a phenomenological study—meaning researchers looked at what it felt like and what it meant for participants to live through something—by Lindsay Branham at the University of Cambridge, researchers considered whether the "internal blueprints" of human attachment theory were also active in people's connection with nature.

A total of 299 participants from the UK and the United States took part through three evaluations, all leveraging scientifically valid and reliable assessments:

- **Interoceptive Awareness.** How skilled were participants at noticing and understanding their internal bodily signals—such as changes in temperature, hunger, and how their body responds to different emotional states? (e.g., "I notice how my body changes when I feel happy.")

- **Relational Attachment.** What is their typical relational attachment style? (Approach-Avoid, Approach-Anxious, Secure)
- **Nature Connectedness.** What is their love and care for nature?

From there, researchers looked for relationships between the three factors, to better understand how they do (or do not) influence one another. Their key findings:

1. **Interoceptive Awareness is Key:** Higher interoceptive skill is a significant predictor of how connected to nature someone will feel.
2. **Emotional Awareness Matters Most:** The "emotional awareness" component of interoception was the strongest predictor. If you are more aware of how your body responds when you feel certain emotions, you're more likely to form a deep, "secure" bond with natural environments.
3. **"Secure Attachment to Nature":** People with higher levels of self-awareness often engage in more pro-environmental behaviors and report higher levels of overall well-being.
4. **Nature as a Reliable "Other":** The research suggests that, for some, nature can function as a secure attachment figure—similar to how a secure human relationship can be a source of co-regulation that lowers heart rate, turns down the volume on stress, and enables restoration.

In summary, this study says that people who are self-aware—emotionally and in their body—usually have a strong bond with nature, and that bond can play the role of a secure attachment that helps you slow down, lower your heart rate, and downregulate your nervous system.

The paper is clear to say that, as of now, the role nature plays is a "mediating role," meaning emotional self-awareness is what bridges your body awareness to your kinship with nature. Instead of just "I feel the wind on my skin," you're able to experience and name: "I belong here and am part of this world."

This all tracks with the research and experience of those at the forefront of *shinrin-yoku*, or "forest bathing," which we'll explore in detail soon: the human-nature bond activates the soothing system—the "rest and digest" parasympathetic nervous response.

Compassion, safety, connection, groundedness—instead of drive, fear, and anxiety.

We don't know whether being self-aware causes you to love nature, or whether spending time in nature causes you to become more self-aware. It's a chicken-or-egg situation. But we do know that being in nature and practicing mindful awareness of ourselves and our environment is good for our mind, body, and spirit. We know it in science and in experience.

So what does it look like to spend time in nature as a practice, a habit, a routine? That's where the rest of this book is heading.

For now, here is a general framework to consider. Created by Rachel Hopman, Ph.D., *The Nature Pyramid* provides a simple, accessible, and sustainable structure for setting down the devices, turning down the volume on tasks and to-dos, and engaging with nature in a tiered way.

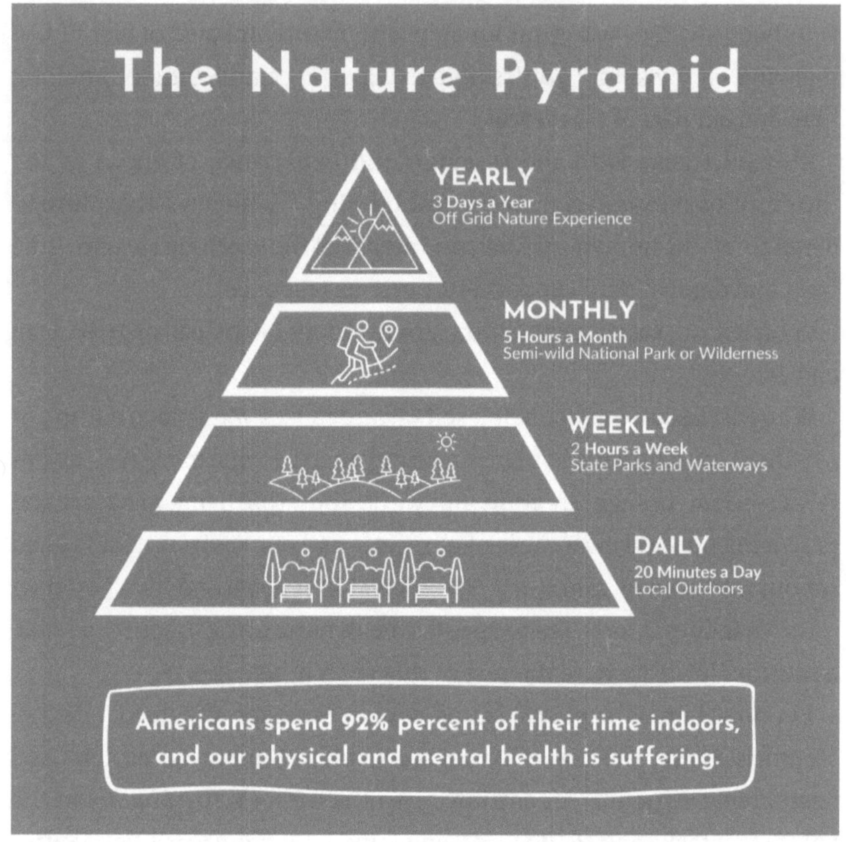


*The Nature Pyramid by Rachel Hopman, Ph.D.*

By breaking nature exposure down into daily 20-minute local doses and monthly backwoods immersions, The Nature Pyramid offers a practical, scalable roadmap for moving back toward a natural baseline of connection. It's a compelling invitation that doesn't require us to "go off grid" or be in deep wilderness every weekend to find restoration; we just need to intentionally weave time outdoors into the fabric of our existing routines—daily, weekly, monthly, and yearly.

* * *

Let me close this chapter with a passage from one of my favorite books in recent years. I haven't historically read a lot of fiction, but at the recommendation of a coworker and friend, I picked up a book in a genre I'd never heard of: solarpunk.

Solarpunk imagines a sustainable future interconnected with nature and community—hopeful, countercultural, regenerative, and rooted in a belief that a different world is possible.

*A Psalm for the Wild-Built* by Becky Chambers tells the story of a tea monk named Dex who, upon wanting to explore the wilderness outside the city, encounters a robot named Mosscap. A hundred years prior, robots had gained sentience and chosen to isolate themselves from humans. As time passed, Mosscap set out on a pilgrimage of sorts— to check in on humans and ask a single question: "What do humans need?"

As they learn more about one another, Dex and Mosscap find them- selves regularly having to slow down to understand how the other sees the world. In one particularly poignant conversation, Mosscap tries to explain how thoroughly backward our assumptions about nature are— that even people who consider themselves deeply in touch with natural cycles still struggle with a fundamental inversion:

*"You will still struggle to understand that human constructs are carved out and overlaid, that these are the places that are the in-between, not the other way around."*

What a beautiful realization—to know that we are in and part of nature, not apart from it. That we are not simply *in* nature, but nature itself. If we allow ourselves to be.

This also brings to mind the essential book *Braiding Sweetgrass* by Potawatomi author Robin Wall Kimmerer. Her beautiful, and at times challenging, book blends scientific inquiry and indigenous wisdom. Kimmerer's way of seeing the world and telling its story has inspired me—even in the writing of this book you are reading now.

In a passage that articulates a central tenet of her understanding, she writes:

> *"One of our responsibilities as human people is to find ways to enter into reciprocity with the more-than-human world. We can do it through gratitude, through ceremony, through land-stewardship, science, art, and in everyday acts of practical reverence."*

We are not *in* nature. We are part of nature.

And being in reciprocity with nature—and ourselves—is both a calling and a responsibility.

# The Science of Being in Nature

*The wilderness constantly reminds me that wholeness is not about perfection.*
— Parker Palmer

* * *

If you're anything like me, you've probably had that moment on a trail or sitting by a lake where you think, "I don't need anyone to tell me this—being outside—is good for me."

You can feel it in the way your shoulders drop an inch, the way your breathing shifts from shallow and mindless to something deep and rhythmic, and the way the to-do list screaming in your head finally lowers its volume to a hum.

But as much as we feel these benefits intuitively, there is a profound, growing body of evidence that proves what's happening isn't just "in our heads." It is happening in our blood, our cells, and our immune systems.

Before I go into the particulars of the science (as a layperson and not an actual scientist), let me explain why I think it's important not to get too caught up in mastering it. I'll explain by talking about tomatoes.

A few summers ago, as I was slicing a tomato I had picked from my garden, I caught myself thinking, "These have lycopene," with lycopene being an antioxidant good for our health, according to doctors and scientists. I had this thought with a certain level of proud remembering—a mental pat on the back about making a good choice in my nutritional habits.

And that's when I decided I hated knowing about lycopene.

I eat tomatoes because they are juicy and sweet, with a little tang. And I can grow my own. They're great in a salad, on a burger, obliterated into salsa, slathered on a pizza crust, and, when they're still green, battered and fried.

That's enough reason to eat a tomato.

I don't ever need to think about lycopene. I'm not eating tomatoes *for* their lycopene. I'm not trying to understand or calculate the nutritional or scientific value of my tomatoes.

I simply want to enjoy them.

How does this relate to the science of being in nature? Because I think we can have too much of a good thing. That is to say, science is good—essential!—but humans and our well-being are more than calculations, nutrition labels, and chemical compounds.

If we're constantly adding to the list of things we need to quantify, calculate, optimize, perfect, consume, and apply to ourselves—how can that lead anywhere other than some measure of perfectionism, obsession, anxiety, and a lingering sense that we could be doing it better? Or that we'll never be satisfied and always fall short?

Thinking about lycopene while I slice and eat tomatoes tempts me into a utilitarian view of my food. Of the world.

That my food is a sum of the nutritional value it provides me.

That food is primarily about calories and nutrients and inputs.

That the value of food is only—or at least primarily—about the molecules and compounds that they provide my body.

That this is a transaction between food and my body, and I can get it right. I can perfect it.

The same goes for spending time in nature. We can end up "majoring in the minors"—focusing on the particulars in a transactional way that distorts or even gets in the way of the true connection we're seeking: with ourselves, nature, or other people.

Spending time doing anything while being solely focused on it being "good for us" and trying to do it perfectly is nothing but a comedy of errors.

Well-being can't be about perfection. Thriving can't be about perfection. That math-like mindset—applying a sense of perfectibility to living a full and grounded life—will leave you void of satisfaction and blaming yourself for falling short.

Perfectionists aren't people who get things perfect. They are people who want perfection and think perfection is attainable. It's a recipe for endless striving, predictable exhaustion, and compounding disappointment. And so I think we all need to count less.

Less counting, less measuring, less optimizing. It's not that we shouldn't care about our health, our habits, our consumption, our impact on ourselves and others and the environment. But is the transactional, perfectionist view of the world actually serving me? You? Us?

For me, I'm going to do what I can to stay open to wonder, curiosity, and learning. I trust that those things will serve me well and perhaps lead to thriving. That's where I see possibilities today.

* * *

Bringing this back to the science of being in nature: it would have been easy enough for me to leave this chapter out, to simply describe the purpose and the pathway to benefiting from nature without breaking it down into science and particles and brain function. I'm including it for a few reasons (and I'm sure there are other good reasons, too):

- **The science can amplify wonder.** Some people will be fully engaged and find a specific experience of awe and wonder as they consider the way our complex minds and bodies engage with our environment. Instead of getting in the way, the science may amplify the experience of time in nature for them.
- **The science can increase confidence.** There are those who are skeptical about practices that may involve walking barefoot in the grass or lying on the forest floor for an hour. Knowing there is evidence-based science that underpins the experiential data helps them open their mind to new possibilities.
- **The science can direct interest.** There may be aspects of the research—on how the immune system, for example, responds to time spent in a forest—that spark specific actions, habits, or "prescriptions" when someone is looking for new ways to promote mental and physical health.

All this to say, as we get into the science: if this is helpful to you, fantastic! If it feels unnecessary, or like an obstacle to your authentic and grounded experience in the forest, *just skip it!*

*One last reminder: I'm not a medical doctor or physician of any kind. You should not take any of the science or practices that follow as medical advice or mental health treatment. Please consult with your own health care professionals before you begin any practices or habits aimed at your mental and physical health.*

## Forest Medicine

In the last few decades, a new field has emerged called "Forest Medicine." What started as a cultural practice in Japan in the 1980s has transformed into a rigorous, interdisciplinary science. Organizations like the Japanese Society of Forest Medicine are now showing that nature isn't just a nice backdrop for a walk—it can be a preventive medicine that helps shield us from, and recover from, many of the mental and physical illnesses of modern, sedentary life.

One of the most fascinating discoveries in this field is that trees are constantly communicating—not just with each other, but with us. They release natural chemical compounds called terpenes or phytoncides— essentially the forest's own aerosol system.

When we walk through a pine forest or a cedar grove, we are literally inhaling particles from the forest's immune system. And when we do, our own immune systems respond in kind.

Researchers, led by pioneers like Dr. Qing Li, have found that inhaling these terpenes activates our "Natural Killer" (NK) cells. These are the frontline soldiers of our immune system, responsible for fighting off infections and even targeting cancerous cells. The most remarkable part? A single afternoon spent in a terpene-rich forest may boost your NK cell activity for up to a week. Studies have shown that a three-day immersion can sustain that boost for up to a month in some cases.

It turns out that "forest bathing" isn't just a metaphor. We are literally bathing our internal systems in a life-giving chemistry.


## Rewiring the Stressed Brain

We've talked about "soft fascination"—that effortless way the brain engages with the play of light through leaves or the rhythm of a stream. Science now has a way to measure the "psychological capital" that it builds.

When we practice forest bathing, we see a statistically significant reduction in what researchers call the "negative five": stress, anxiety, depression, anger, and confusion. By inhaling those same terpenes we mentioned earlier, our cortisol levels—the "stress hormone"—begin to drop. But it goes deeper than just cortisol; studies show a measurable decrease in adrenaline and noradrenaline, the chemical markers of a body in high-alert mode.

This shifts us out of the "fight or flight" sympathetic nervous system and into the "rest and digest" parasympathetic system. This is a crucial shift for anyone who struggles with rumination—that loop of repetitive, negative thoughts. Nature acts as a circuit breaker, quieting the parts of the brain that over-analyze and judge, and instead boosting our vigor and mental clarity.

But it's not just about what goes down; it's about what goes up. Nature connection is closely linked to "eudaimonic well-being"—a scientific term for a sense of vitality and meaning. It's the difference between just "not being stressed" and actually feeling alive, creative, and purposeful.

## Heart-Deep Health

Beyond the brain, nature attends to the heart. Research supports the cardiovascular benefits of spending time in the woods. We see significant reductions in blood pressure, pulse rate, and heart rate. This isn't just about feeling relaxed in the moment. These changes suggest a powerful preventive effect against hypertension and heart disease.

It's as if the steady, slow rhythm of the natural world invites our own internal systems to pace themselves. In an era where we are constantly "optimized" toward more productivity (and a higher heart rate), nature offers the opposite: a return to a healthy, sustainable baseline.

## The Chemistry of Well-being

Perhaps most exciting is the way nature exposure may alter our internal pharmacy. Emerging research has identified that forest bathing can increase blood levels of several key "feel-good" markers:

- **Serotonin:** For those not taking antidepressants, nature can naturally boost this mood-regulating neurotransmitter.
- **Oxytocin:** Often called the "bonding hormone," its increase helps us feel more connected—not just to the environment, but to ourselves and others.
- **IGF-1 (Insulin-like Growth Factor I):** Important for mood regulation, with potent antidepressant effects.

We aren't just looking at trees; we are undergoing a systemic chemical recalibration.

And if you've ever found yourself sleeping more soundly after a day in the woods, the science backs you up. Forest bathing has been shown to improve subjective sleep quality and increase sleep length. By helping to regulate our nervous system during the day, nature allows our bodies to actually let go at night—offering a natural remedy for the sleep disorders that plague our screen-filled lives.

## Our "Old Friends" in the Soil

If you've ever felt a strange sense of joy just by getting your hands in the garden or sitting on the bare ground, you can thank an "old friend" named *Mycobacterium vaccae*.

This is a harmless but beneficial microbe found in healthy soil. When we are exposed to it—through touch or even by breathing it in while we're near the earth—researchers have found that it stimulates the production of serotonin in animal models, suggesting there could be human benefits as well. The findings are at the forefront of neurobiological studies. It's a reminder that we are, quite literally, made of the same stuff as the earth.

Because of these broad physiological shifts, forest medicine is being explored as a legitimate path for rehabilitation and disease prevention. Studies indicate that it can reduce pain and anxiety for cancer patients, improve quality of life for menopausal women, and even help individuals with asthma or atopic dermatitis. Remarkably, hospital patients with a view of trees or proximity to a forest have been shown to recover faster and require less pain medication than those staring at a brick wall.

The science of forest therapy suggests that the healing we feel isn't caused by just one thing. It is the "total effect" of all five senses being stimulated in a non-demanding way:

- **Sight:** Our eyes are drawn to fractals—the repetitive, complex patterns found in fern fronds, snowflakes, and tree branches. These patterns are visually "easy" for our brains to process, which creates an immediate sense of relaxation.
- **Sound:** The frequency of birdsong or a bubbling brook has been shown to help the brain recover from "directed attention fatigue."
- **Touch:** Even the act of touching wood or bark has been shown to induce significant physiological relaxation, lowering blood pressure and pulse rates.
- **Smell and Taste:** As we've seen, inhaling the forest's scent regulates our hormone secretion and balances our nervous system.

## A Practice for Life

As we move through the practices in the following chapters, keep this science in the back of your mind. You don't have to think about NK cells or terpenes while you're out there—in fact, I'd prefer you didn't! But you can trust that while you are slowing down to notice the moss or the wind, your body is doing the quiet, scientific work of returning to itself.

# Shinrin-Yoku: Forest Bathing 101

*"What if we saw the wounded earth not as a thing to steward,
but an integrated being of which we are part?"*
— Michele Dunne, OFS

* * *

You might be tempted, at first glance, to think that forest bathing is another woo-woo, granola-loving, tree-hugging ritual that someone came up with while using medicinal drugs in a yurt— it's so much better than that.

And to be clear, it does not involve a bathtub. People have sincerely asked me.

"Forest bathing" is a literal translation of the Japanese term *shinrin-yoku.*

In the early 1980s, Japanese doctors began prescribing time in the forests of the island nation to remedy the increasing prevalence of maladies and illnesses that came along with sedentary, office-based knowledge work (as opposed to physical labor).

The prescription was essentially to go spend slow, intentional, mindful time amongst the trees.

In the five decades since, evidence-based researchers, doctors, and scientists have been studying the effects of this intentional, mindful time in nature—of forest bathing. The previous chapter went into detail on the scientific research showing the real mental, physical, emotional, and spiritual benefits. Suffice it to say for now: the benefits are real and lasting.

So what exactly does forest bathing entail?

First off, it's not hiking.  So if you hate the idea of slinging on a backpack, carrying everything you need for survival, and double-checking the elevation gain of a particular trail—you're safe. We aren't doing any of that in forest bathing.

Where hiking is often focused on getting to a certain destination, completing a particular distance, or accomplishing a feat—forest bathing is satisfyingly simplistic.

Here is how I describe forest bathing:

> Taking time to slowly immerse yourself in the experience of nature by mindfully using all of your senses to notice, appreciate, and connect—with nature and yourself.

"That's it?" Yes. The simplicity is relieving.

I'll share several practices here as starting points for forest bathing. But know that one of the greatest strengths of this as a practice is that it doesn't require memorizing detailed techniques, following rigid structures, or complex theory.

The simplest invitation into forest bathing is this: "What do you notice?"

* * *

I want to take a few minutes to thoughtfully break down—to annotate, in a way—the definition of forest bathing I just introduced.

*Taking time to slowly immerse yourself in the experience of nature by mindfully using all of your senses to notice, appreciate, and connect—with nature and yourself.*

*Taking time to slowly immerse yourself...*

How often do you truly slow down? The pace of modern life, even when it might be described as "relaxed," is very rarely slow. Taking time to slowly immerse in nature means letting go of your default speed setting. It means being uncomfortable at first (and maybe for a while longer) as your nervous system tries to figure out: "What's wrong? Why aren't we going faster? Why aren't we solving problems?"

To slow down means we get to see things differently. Instead of, metaphorically, looking out the car window to see a blur as everything flies by, we can notice more—and notice more detail.

*...in the experience of nature...*

Nature is not simply a place. It is an experience. The goal of an experience isn't to learn facts about it, nor is it simply to gather data points to recite later. An experience has to be had. And since we are part of nature (not just in nature), we are part of the experience we are having as well. *You are nature having an experience of nature while in nature!* As we slow down for this experience, we encounter an unexpected, perhaps new way of experiencing both nature and ourselves.

*...by mindfully using all of your senses...*

I'll admit: my first instinct when spending time along the river or in a state park is to take pictures. Whether it's with my phone or the fancy new "professional" camera I bought in early 2025, I love nature photography. It's purely a hobby at this point—a creative release that allows me to share my experience with others after the fact.

But seeing nature through a camera isn't the same as really observing with my eyes what's present along the trail or in the garden.

Using all of my senses—sight, hearing, touch, smell, and taste—opens up virtually endless opportunities to experience my environment.

Sure, if you're on a hike and you pass through a cluster of pine trees, you're likely to notice and maybe even say out loud, "It smells like Christmas out here." But otherwise, you aren't likely to be mindfully engaging with your sense of smell. And your sense of touch might be limited to just the feel of the trail under your shoes.

Our senses help us interact with and understand our environment. And as you'll read in the science chapter, there is enormous invisible benefit to physical and mental health from engaging in mindful breathing while in nature.

*...to notice, appreciate, and connect—with nature and yourself.*

When we slow down to engage with our environment through all of our senses, we can have so many more rich emotional moments—curiosity, wonder, awe, and delight—that we would otherwise miss.

I was on a short walk in the woods just yesterday, amongst yellow and orange and red leaves in the canopy and all over the forest floor. I decided to lie down and look straight up, just to have a new vantage point of the trees.

As soon as I settled in on my back, I noticed a sweet smell—likely from the sugars breaking down in the leaves. I felt the dry, crisp crunch of the leaves under the palms of my hands. I noticed how firm and supportive the ground was beneath my back. And all of this brought a warm smile to my face. The joy came from a sense of playfulness in doing something I don't normally do in my daily life (lying on the forest floor) and from the sense of connection to the world around me—as well as the connection to a part of me that felt new, interesting, and pleasant. *Noticing, appreciating, and connecting...to nature and myself.*

## How to Practice Forest Bathing

As a practice, forest bathing can be an individual or group experience. You can self-guide or work with a certified forest bathing or forest therapy guide.

Oftentimes, a forest bathing session with a certified guide will be two hours or more. There are evidence-based reasons for this, and it's also simply true that it takes time to slow down and create space to practice intentionally connecting—especially if this is an entirely new way of being in the world for you. Rushing or cramming in an experience will negate the calming, restorative effects you hope to gain during a session.

From here, I'll describe how I run a two-hour group session. After that, I'll offer a few tips on how you could self-guide an individual experience.

### Grounding

Even if you're coming into a forest bathing session from a place of ease and calm, it's important to help your whole self—mind, body, and spirit—find a grounded place to start from. How much more so if you're feeling tired, frazzled, disorganized, or stressed.

I begin with a five- to seven-minute exercise of mindfulness—a combination of intentional breathing and a body scan.

Participants are invited to find a comfortable way to sit or lie down and close their eyes if that feels right and helps them focus. We then do a few rounds of simple box breathing—four counts in, hold for four, four counts out, hold for four. I start with deep breaths, then invite them to continue the breathing in whatever way feels comfortable.

The invitation then becomes to simply notice and observe the breath—not to change it or force it, but just to get comfortable feeling it and being aware of the rhythm, the sensation, and the experience. (You can start to see how this sets the stage for how we'll engage with the forest and with ourselves once we're grounded and using all of our senses.)

A body scan then follows, which simply takes our attention and uses it to notice our whole body, starting at the top of the head and scanning down to the tips of our toes. Again, the goal isn't to change anything—but simply to notice. Where is there tension? Where is there ease? Temperature, weight, connection to the ground or chair. Simply observing and accepting what is.

Before coming back into the space, we do another minute or so of simply noticing our breath. Then I invite participants, when they are ready, to open their eyes and come back into the space. Often there are warm smiles, maybe a deep breath of appreciation, or a stretching of the arms and back.

Now we are grounded and moving toward the slow immersion we are here for.

## Intention

It's important to note at this point that forest bathing doesn't have a goal, necessarily. Not in the same way going to a workshop on time management or taking a weightlifting class might. We do intend for forest bathing to have a positive impact on us—but we aren't pursuing a particular outcome per se, beyond slowly immersing yourself in the experience of nature, as we outlined in the definition. (And even that is wildly subjective—because you could experience a lot of distraction and disruption, from yourself, others, or the environment, and still find it to be a beneficial experience. Just as in a mindfulness or meditation practice, "perfect" doesn't exist. Always becoming, never arriving.)

I do think it's valuable to hold an intention loosely, however.

After the grounding, participants are invited to share anything that feels right about their intention for the session. I often say something along the lines of:

*"This is a time for you to share what brought you here and how you hope to experience yourself during our time together today."*

Notice that I didn't say "What do you hope to get from this time?" or "What do you want to walk away having learned today?"

I trust that those who show up authentically will get something and learn something—but it's not important to be so direct in your intentions.

Oftentimes participants will say things like, "I just want to relax" or "I'm hoping to feel calm and less stressed out." Part of my approach, as a forest bathing guide and as a coach, is to allow people to name what feels true for them without overidentifying with those thoughts, ideas, or sentiments. That's why I try not to add commentary, correct, or even remind people of the intentions they may share. It's enough to name them and then allow them to drift away from our conscious thinking.

After all, forest bathing isn't a thinking experience—you aren't trying to memorize the names of birds, identify the trees, or understand the biology of the ecosystem. This is a different kind of knowing we are working with.

I'll say that one more time: forest bathing isn't a thinking-based experience. The goal isn't to come away with new thoughts, clearer thoughts, or better thoughts. We aren't trying to *get* something from nature—certainly not textbook information. We want, to the best of our ability, to reconnect with nature and ourselves in a way that surpasses the head knowledge we tend to prioritize in our everyday lives.

**Practices**

The simplest way to describe the practices of forest bathing is this: take fifteen minutes and use one of your senses to explore, be curious, notice, observe, and absorb what is around you—above, below, nearby, far away.

You can do this sitting on the ground, leaning against a tree, lying on your back, or slowly meandering on a path or through a clearing (assuming it's safe and allowed where you are).

There is no right or wrong order for moving through the senses. I tend to prefer this order:

- **Sight** is the most familiar and typically the most comfortable way for most people to start.
- **Sound** tends to bring up a certain level of "I never realized!"
- **Smell** can feel challenging for some, as many people are accustomed to artificial or heavily sweet smells.
- **Feel** opens people back up, and they often have a clearer vocabulary to describe their experiences.
- **Taste** is a powerful way to close out (and I'll talk more about ways to do this), though it can be the toughest to create or experience safely.

Any forest bathing session can weave through the senses in any order, even doubling back to revisit one from a new perspective. It's really just a matter of time and creativity in designing a session.

Let me give you some specific prompts or invitations I might use for each of the senses. This way you'll have a clearer picture of what to expect, and some ideas for how to self-guide.

Any single prompt below could be sufficient to set someone up for a successful practice, while it can also be helpful to provide two or three "ways in" for those who are new to this kind of practice.

**Sight**
- What do you see?
- Notice movement and stillness.
- Notice the full spectrum of colors around you.
- Look up. Look down.
- Notice along the horizon or at a distance.

**Sound**

- What do you hear?
- Listen for rhythm and volume.
- Listen for the invisible.
- Listen for the visible.
- Listen by cupping your ears to amplify or direct sound.

**Smell**
- What do you smell?
- Smell for what is sweet or pungent.
- Smell for moisture or dryness.
- Smell for ripeness, decay, or newness.
- Smell with your eyes closed.

**Feel**
- What do you feel?
- Touch for texture.
- Touch for weight and density.
- Touch with your hands, your feet, your toes, your skin.
- Touch with your eyes closed.

**Taste**
- What do you taste?
- *Important:* only taste what you know to be 100% safe.
- Taste water from a flowing stream or spring.
- Taste a store-bought fruit native to your environment.
- Taste tea or another beverage with an ingredient native to your environment.

**Follow and Let Go**

I also like to invite people, after having experienced the forest through each of the senses individually, to take one additional span of time to follow their senses and interweave them, play with them, and fully explore whatever comes up.

This can happen as you stroll slowly back to a starting point, or by inviting folks to "have a sit"—placing themselves in a spot that allows them to do nothing, be responsible for nothing, and experience whatever they find their mind, body, or spirit moving toward. In some ways, this is a release from focusing—allowing the proverbial clouds to pass through the sky without attaching to them or trying to keep them in place.

**Completion**

Closing out an experience like forest bathing is one more opportunity to connect and integrate—with yourself and with nature. Instead of dusting off your hands and hopping back into the car, take a few additional minutes to reflect and absorb your experience.

In my first true forest bathing experience, led by a skillful guide who has now become a friend and collaborator, our completion exercise was centered around a blanket spread on the ground, with sticks, acorns, pinecones, and leaves artfully laid out into a lovely design. Placed as the centerpiece, small hand-thrown mugs sat ready to be filled with ginger tea. Small wooden bowls held tasty treats and seasonal fruits. Bringing food and drink into the experience was a way to "bathe" in the tastes of the forest—as well as tapping into the ritual of a shared meal that humans have practiced for millennia.

Reflection questions or prompts can be offered to the group as well:

- How was this experience for you?
- What did you notice about yourself throughout the session?
- What emotions did you experience?
- How does it feel to be you right now?
- What are you grateful for in this moment?

· What are you carrying with you as we leave here today?

I avoid the temptation to make an explicit call to "put this into practice every day," simply because the goal of a forest bathing session isn't to optimize it, perfect it, automate it, or systematize it. While of course there can be takeaways that shape and change the way we move through our days (yes!), the most beneficial practice of forest bathing is about being present to the moment and reconnecting with yourself and with nature—without the expectation that this is a transaction you are simply going through.

**The goal is grounding, not extraction. Connecting, not obtaining. Practicing, not mastering.**

Some may find it beneficial to journal about their experience, to share stories with a partner or friend, or even to snap a few photos during a session to share on social media. (I think it's okay to take a photo here or there during a session—mindfully and in limited numbers—even though technology can be both a hindrance to mindfulness and a distraction that shifts your intention in forest bathing.)

## Self-Guided Forest Bathing

The beauty of this practice is that you don't really need specialized training or expertise. While it can be nice to learn from a skillful guide, and it can be beneficial to share experiences with a group, the reality is that you're fully capable of creating an experience of connecting with nature on your own.

A few tips that may help:

· **Let someone know where you're going and how long you'll be there.** This is basic outdoors safety, as well as an opportunity to come back and share a little about your experience—the way you might during a completion exercise with a group.

- **Jot down a short list of practices or your preferred order.** You don't have to memorize anything to go forest bathing. Even if it feels overly simple, write down a quick order of steps you want to go through, so you don't have to worry about forgetting—and to keep you honest about the intentions you set as you start.

- **Use a simple timer to help create structure.** A simple (non-smart) watch if you can. Or a kitchen timer. A smartphone is fine, so long as you aren't tempted to read notifications or check messages. Having something to help you track the passing of time—ten or fifteen minutes per exercise—can give you permission to fully release into the practice and ensure you give yourself the space to fully lean in.

- **Adapt to your needs and desires.** You likely know what you need to create a positive experience. Maybe you can't stand for long periods, or you need to have a snack or drink on hand for blood sugar. Don't give in to trying to do something you think you "should" do—be gentle, empathetic, and intentional in caring for yourself.

- **Don't cut your time short.** It's tempting when you're on your own to cut corners, rush the clock, or simply skip parts of the process. Honor yourself by slowing down and practicing.

- **The case for practicing in the same place.** You may think that forest bathing in the same location too often would grow stale—because you'll already know everything there is to know about that environment. Challenge accepted! It's true that a new trail, forest, or park may be easier to engage with fresh eyes. But as the Buddhist saying goes, "You can never step in the same river twice, for you have changed and so has the river." I love the idea of consistently showing up to the same location and having new experiences—because it teaches me, over and over, that I can always experience places, people, ideas, and things with fresh eyes. That I should continue to be curious about all things, no matter how familiar they may seem. Of course you can and should explore new places! And see what comes from showing up to the same place, consistently.

## Don't have two hours for a true forest bath?

**5-4-3-2-1**

This practice, dating back to the 1990s and credited to psychotherapist Betty Alice Erickson, was originally focused on helping people experiencing intense anxiety or even panic attacks. As a grounding exercise, it allows a person to use their surrounding environment to ground themselves in a sense of safety, calming the nervous system and regulating intense emotions.

The beautiful thing about this simple technique is that we can also use it to promote positive emotions, awareness, and connection—without having to be in a state of anxiety, panic, or other distress. You don't have to be sick in order to get healthier.

Take a minute to find a comfortable place to sit in a natural environment. Notice your breathing and take a few intentional breaths to help yourself be present to this moment. Then notice...

- **5** things you can see
- **4** things you can touch
- **3** things you can hear
- **2** things you can smell
- **1** thing you can taste

Just as you would in a forest bathing session, take time to notice without judgment or overanalysis. Notice, be curious, and absorb the experience. You don't have to be in a natural environment to benefit—but being in and around nature will bring greater benefits.

## Where to Find a Certified Forest Therapy Spaces

The best location is the one you're most likely to go to. It's that simple.

At the same time, just as in Japan, the United States has a growing number of places certified by the Association of Nature & Forest Therapy Guides and Programs. Their website reads:

> *Certified Forest Therapy trails are carefully curated paths that invite you to slow down, breathe deeply, and reconnect with the natural world. These trails are scattered across the globe, each offering a unique blend of flora, fauna, and landscapes that inspire tranquility and mindfulness.*

There are currently 14 ANFT-Certified Trails, Spaces, or Places— locations that have met rigorous criteria for safety, ecological health, and therapeutic design. You can find the current list at: www.anft.earth/ trails-overview/

# No Bad Weather

*Dearest, I beg of you, sleep properly and go for walks.*
— Franz Kafka

*In nature, nothing is perfect and everything is perfect.*
*Trees can be contorted, bent in weird ways, and they're still beautiful.*
— Alice Walker

* * *

Where forest bathing is a specific practice aimed at slowing down and reconnecting with nature and yourself—not every moment you spend outdoors needs to be a devoted mindfulness session with deep sensory experiences.

If we zoom back out to a broader perspective on the benefits of being in nature, we find still more opportunity to practice being in and part of nature—by considering that we don't need ideal conditions to get outside.

Depending on where you live, you might have found yourself saying it's too cold or too hot, too rainy or too snowy, to spend any substantial amount of time outdoors.

In the 2017 book *There's No Such Thing as Bad Weather: A Scandinavian Mom's Secrets for Raising Healthy, Resilient, and Confident Kids,* Linda

Åkeson McGurk presents a compelling perspective on how Americans might benefit from learning how other cultures embrace less-than-ideal weather.

The title comes from a Swedish proverb: "There's no such thing as bad weather, only bad clothes."

If you're uncomfortable in the weather, you aren't prepared. "Whose fault is that?" the proverb seems to slyly suggest.

The book is a beautiful, necessary, and at times convicting reminder that our disconnection from the outdoors isn't usually a problem with nature itself, but with our own expectations and hyper-convenient, modern, climate-controlled comfort zones. *No Such Thing as Bad Weather* is where I learned the Norwegian term *friluftsliv*—coined by poet and playwright Henrik Ibsen in 1859, meaning "open-air life." *Friluftsliv* is about embracing a year-round connection with nature, regardless of weather. And you can imagine the weather that Norway experiences at certain times of the year.

> *"In Sweden, nature is not an abstract concept that is taught only on Earth Day and through textbooks about bees and butterflies. It's an integral part of everyday life. Daily interaction with nature has helped turn many children, myself included, into passionate advocates for the environment."*

The ripple effect of having an integrated relationship with nature extends beyond the individual into broader society—implications that should be fully considered in a world with a rapidly shifting climate because of human choices.

*No Such Thing as Bad Weather* and *friluftsliv* aren't about just being rugged and toughening up—but embracing a playful, grounded, and appropriately prepared mental and physical engagement with the world around us.

In all of this, I'm reminded of my good friends Tyler and Erin. With their two young daughters, they tapped into this very mindset when they took on the 1000 Hours Outside challenge.

Created by Ginny Yurich, a mother of five and former teacher from Michigan, *1000 Hours Outside* has become a movement in its own right. Through her own experiences and experiments with taking her five kids outside for extended periods of time, Yurich found they would play more creatively and get along better—in addition to sleeping more soundly at night—when they spent extended time outdoors. She eventually chose a target—1,000 hours a year—because it roughly mirrored the average amount of time American children spend in front of screens each year (which, let's be honest, has likely only increased in the years since she launched her movement).

Erin and Tyler have taken on this challenge several years in a row, not always hitting the exact 1,000 hours—but they will passionately tell you that the experience of trying to spend that time outdoors has made a huge difference in the lives of their daughters. Whether it's a 20-degree day in February or a 90-degree August afternoon, they've found creative ways to tap into their kids' inner resilience and their own sense of creativity to consistently get outdoors.

At times, they invite friends to join their family on "playground tours," taking entire Saturdays to park-hop. Packing lunches and piling into the van, the family adventure requires some patience and flexibility—but the focus is on being outside and doing it together.

Erin has shared countless times over the years when her daughters fought against going outside—especially when the weather was less than ideal or they felt tired. But time and time again, she says, once they get outside, everything changes. They play, coming up with new games or ways of exploring their own backyard, and their energy (and attitudes) rise above the conditions. Puddles become oceans, snowdrifts become igloos, sticks become wands, and trees become forts.

And if you're thinking "1,000 hours outdoors in a year—which is roughly 19 hours per week, or about 2 hours and 45 minutes a day— sounds impossible," or that it's just another data-tracking, life-hacking, measurable outcome to optimize, the *1000 Hours Outside* website acknowledges the tension:

> *We certainly are not militant about it and we don't take a 'no screens ever or you will surely die' approach either. But we would, quite vehemently, argue that nature—big, beautiful, bountiful nature—is the absolute and very BEST reprieve for you and your children. Honestly, they don't even compare!*

In the years Erin and Tyler have set the 1,000-hour goal for their kids, they've only hit the target once. But they have zero regrets and plenty of confidence that the routine, habit, and mindset of getting outdoors has greatly benefited their daughters.

* * *

If you want to take on a mindset of *friluftsliv*, here are just a few ideas for working time outdoors—and away from screens or other distractions— into your life. From the small to the more committed, *friluftsliv* can be almost anything that gets you outdoors and connecting with your surroundings. The key is to be slow, unhurried, "leave no trace," and keep it simple (little to no cost or extensive planning).

- Taking a walk in the woods or a city park
- Eating a meal outside, even if it's just a sandwich on a bench
- Drinking your morning coffee outdoors
- Biking—to work or simply for pleasure
- Sitting by a campfire

- Sleeping in a hammock in your backyard
- Hiking or trekking
- Cross-country skiing or snowshoeing
- Visiting a body of water (stream, lake, river, ocean)
- Picking wild berries or hunting mushrooms
- Fishing, canoeing, or kayaking
- Nature photography (leisurely)
- Camping in a tent or a simple cabin
- Building a snowman or snow castle
- Practicing grounding or "earthing" each morning by making direct skin contact with the earth—such as walking barefoot on grass or soil
- Gardening (or container gardening if you're tight on space)
- Creating nature art using found elements—pinecones, flowers, pebbles

The best activities to do outdoors are the ones you will actually enjoy. Don't force yourself into something you think you are *supposed* to be doing. Do experiments and give new experiences a chance. In the end, though, building a nature-connected life will come from a place of authentic connection, not rigid compliance.

# Instructions for Living a Life

*There is in all visible things—a hidden wholeness.*
— Thomas Merton

*"When it's over, I want to say: all my life / I was a bride married to amazement."*
— Mary Oliver

* * *

One of the reasons I wanted to write this book was to tap into a larger story—one that goes beyond the finite machinations of our always-on, always-maximizing cultural narrative. Personally, I love the feeling of being in nature, especially when it stops being something I am *doing* and becomes something I am *experiencing*. Every state park hike or city park stroll begins with a clear line: me, the walker and problem-solver, and then the setting—the forest or dirt path. But with practice, intention, and openness to being and experiencing something more, the two become one.

To get nerdy again for a moment—with psychology, specifically—it brings to mind the work of Scott Barry Kaufman and David Yaden, and what they call the *Unitary Continuum*.

## The Unitary Continuum

### Increasing Degrees of Perceived Unity

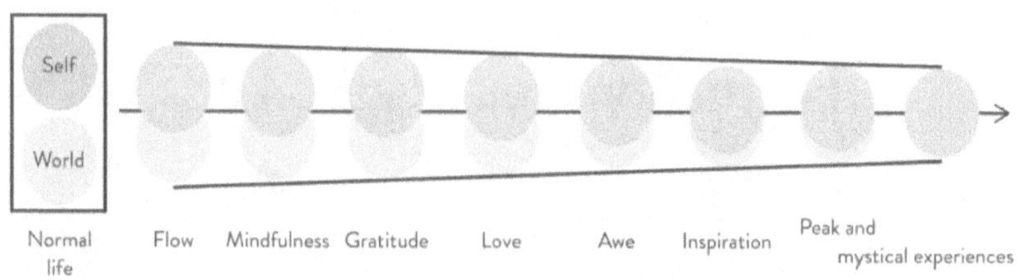


**This conceptual graph was adapted from Yaden et al. (2017), "The Varieties of Self-Transcendent Experience." It suggests a range of transcendent experiences with varying levels of connection with the world and is included for suggestive, demonstrative purposes. Further research is required to further flesh out this model.**

The continuum starts with two separate circles: the Self and the World. That's where most of us live. We are subjects looking at objects. We see a tree as a "thing" to be identified or a trail as a "task" to be completed. This is the realm of "Normal Life," but it's also the realm of isolation.

But as we slow down—as we engage in the soft fascination and sensory immersion of forest bathing—those two circles begin to slide toward each other. The further we move to the right, the more those boundaries dissolve.

- **Flow:** Maybe you're walking and you lose track of time. You aren't "trying" to walk anymore; the walking is just happening.
- **Awe:** You look up at a two-hundred-year-old sycamore, and for a split second, your own ego, your own "small" problems, seem to vanish. You feel a sense of vastness.
- **The Unitive State:** At the far right of the continuum are "peak and mystical experiences." The overlap is complete. You no longer feel like a visitor in the woods. You feel, quite literally, like a part of the

ecosystem. Maybe this is even what I was experiencing at Conner Prairie, when my younger self and present self were present to each other during that first guided forest bathing session.

## Why Nature Makes Transcendence Possible

Kaufman has done remarkable work building on the unfinished legacy of Abraham Maslow. Most people know Maslow's "Hierarchy of Needs" as a pyramid—but Maslow never actually drew it that way (marketers did), and more importantly, he came to believe that self-actualization wasn't the endpoint. In an unpublished 1966 essay, he wrote:

> *"It must be stated that self-actualization is not enough. Personal salvation and what is good for the person alone cannot be really understood in isolation. ... The good of other people must be invoked, as well as the good for oneself. ... It is quite clear that a purely intrapsychic, individualistic psychology, without reference to other people and social conditions, is not adequate."*

This is why Kaufman reimagines the hierarchy not as a pyramid but as a sailboat. The hull—security, connection, self-esteem—keeps you afloat. But the sail—exploration, love, purpose—is what catches the wind. Security is necessary, but growth is what moves you forward. (I wholeheartedly recommend his book, *Transcend*, for the full picture.)

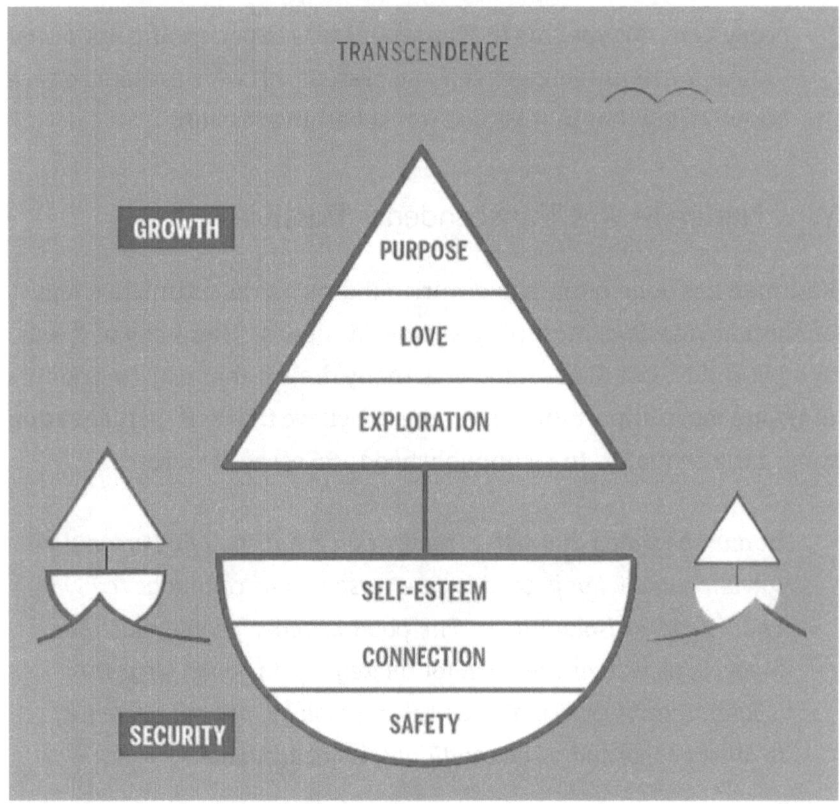



*Adapted from Scott Barry Kaufman's Transcend*

So, back to our purposes here: nature, and walking our problems, and finding space to free ourselves from optimizing and maximizing and living behind our screens.

This is why I believe nature is a necessary and accessible "laboratory" for transcendence. As I wrote earlier, *when I'm in the woods, I'm surrounded by something larger than myself and I'm not responsible for any of it.* That release of responsibility is a shortcut to security. Nature doesn't judge our performance or ask for our résumé. It just provides the holding space.

When we let go of the need to optimize our 20-minute walk, we undermine the need to be the "manager" of our lives and start being a *participant* in life itself. We move from that first box of "Normal Life" into a space where we realize that the "Self" and the "World" were never actually separate to begin with.

We aren't just walking through the problems; we are walking back into the realization that we belong to a whole that is much larger, much older, and much more resilient than our individual worries.

It's not exactly what the farmer-poet Wendell Berry is pointing to when he says, "Whether we and our politicians know it or not, Nature is party to all our deals and decisions, and she has more votes, a longer memory, and a sterner sense of justice than we do."

But the essence of what he's saying is apparent and related.

We aren't people who go *into* nature. We are part of nature. And by connecting—and reconnecting—with nature, we can become more fully human. And when we are more fully human, we can not only experience ourselves in healthier, more sustainable, and more actualized ways—we can self-transcend and begin to more authentically contribute to the good of other people and the world around us.

* * *

Let me close by sharing my favorite lines from the poet Mary Oliver. She quickly became my favorite poet when I read a collection of her work, *Devotion*. (Maybe you've noticed my love for her words leaking out in my writing, as I've obviously already included a few excerpts throughout this book.)

I fell in love with the simplicity of her language, the relaxed and grounded tone of her voice, and the unassuming awe she has when observing the world around her.

These four lines, in essence, have become my mantra for life. They sum up so clearly and succinctly what it is I think I'm here for—perhaps what we are all here to do—as part of nature and in our connection with others.

*Instructions for living a life.*
    *Pay attention.*
    *Be astonished.*
    *Tell about it.*

# ACKNOWLEDGMENTS

Stacey, who believed in me no matter how many times I changed jobs, no matter how many half-baked ideas I was ready to launch, no matter the need to move cross-country while we were growing our family (twice). You will forever be with me—on my walks, in the woods, near the water, and in every moment in between.

My kids, for enduring my insistence on spending Father's Day at Mounds State Park, for being patient with my countless walks, and for tolerating endless nature photo slideshows. I hope someday you'll understand why I kept dragging you outside.

My Weston family. From my great-grandfather, Louis, whose Sunday walks inspired me long before I sat down to write this book, to my great-grandma Cleoyn and grandma Margaret—you, more than any other part of my heritage, taught me to be part of nature, to play in nature, to take care of nature, and to share nature.

Michelle, for being a wise and trusted guide during my first forest bathing experience—and for creating the space where my eleven-year-old self could show up uninvited in a sunflower field.

Nicole, Lindsay, Neli, and Lynnette, for being the best of friends and coaches, even in seasons of change. You've walked alongside me in more ways than one.

Lilach, my Brooklyn-dwelling, voice-memo-sharing friend and confidant. Your presence across the miles has meant more than you know.

My coaching mentors, Laura and Joshua, for believing in me, holding space, and seeing me—truly seeing me—in my work.

Red-tail Land Conservancy, for being faithful stewards of the land in central Indiana and for hosting so many of my outdoor walks and silent conversations. Munsee Woods and the trails you protect have shaped this book as much as any page I've written.

Shafer Leadership Academy, for our partnership and for trusting me to lead "Walk Your Problems" as an experiential leadership workshop. Thank you for taking a chance on slow, grounded work in a world that tends to move too fast.

And to anyone who has ever taken a walk with me—literally or metaphorically—thank you for slowing down with me so we could notice what's around us.

# ABOUT THE AUTHOR

Adam Bouse is a coach, writer, emotions educator, and a possibilitarian.

Before coaching, he worked in museums, tech companies, nonprofits, and communications—always drawn to helping people learn and grow.

In 2025, Adam's family experienced the devastating loss of his wife, Stacey. As cliché as it sounds, grief has a way of making your values abundantly clear. What became clear for Adam is this: grief can live alongside purpose and possibility. And the work that matters most is showing up fully present, creating space where people feel truly heard and seen. Helping people who feel overwhelmed, burned out, and stuck find possibilities, live with intentionality, and discover fulfillment.

Adam is the founder of Optimistic Coaching. He is an International Coaching Federation (ICF) coach, a certified forest therapy guide, and a nature connection specialist. He provides traditional 1:1 coaching and workshops, while also creating experiences that help people reconnect with themselves and the natural world. He writes regularly on Substack about nature, optimism, and resilience, and believes that a walk in the woods is a good place to start solving almost any challenge.

He's inspired by the wisdom of Mary Oliver, Parker Palmer, Richard Rohr, and many others. When he's not coaching, you'll find him outdoors with his camera, hanging out with his kids, or trying to work through his ever-growing "emotional support pile of books."

# SOURCES & FURTHER READING

This book draws on research, writing, and wisdom from many sources. If something here resonated with you, these are good places to keep exploring.

**On Nature, Forest Bathing, and Why It All Matters**
Kimmerer, Robin Wall. *Braiding Sweetgrass: Indigenous Wisdom, Scientific Knowledge, and the Teachings of Plants.* Milkweed Editions, 2013.
Li, Qing. *Forest Bathing: How Trees Can Help You Find Health and Happiness.* Viking, 2018.
McGurk, Linda Åkeson. *There's No Such Thing as Bad Weather: A Scandinavian Mom's Secrets for Raising Healthy, Resilient, and Confident Kids.* Touchstone, 2017.
Offerman, Nick. *Where the Deer and the Antelope Play: The Pastoral Observations of One Ignorant American Who Loves to Walk Outside.* Dutton, 2021.
Tallamy, Douglas W. *Nature's Best Hope: A New Approach to Conservation That Starts in Your Yard.* Timber Press, 2019.
Williams, Florence. *The Nature Fix: Why Nature Makes Us Happier, Healthier, and More Creative.* W.W. Norton & Company, 2017.
Wohlleben, Peter. *The Hidden Life of Trees: What They Feel, How They Communicate.* Greystone Books, 2016.
Association of Nature & Forest Therapy Guides and Programs: www.natureandforesttherapy.earth

## On Attention, Walking, and Being Human

Dillard, Annie. *The Writing Life.* Harper Perennial, 1989.

Kaplan, Rachel, and Stephen Kaplan. *The Experience of Nature: A Psychological Perspective.* Cambridge University Press, 1989.

Thoreau, Henry David. "Walking." *The Atlantic,* June 1862.

Zomorodi, Manoush. *Bored and Brilliant: How Spacing Out Can Unlock Your Most Productive and Creative Self.* St. Martin's Press, 2017.

Zomorodi, Manoush. *Body Electric: The Hidden Costs of the Digital Age and the New Science to Reclaim Your Well-Being.* Harper Wave, 2026.

## On Growth, Transcendence, and Living With Meaning

Chambers, Becky. *A Psalm for the Wild-Built.* Tordotcom, 2021.

Kaufman, Scott Barry. *Transcend: The New Science of Self-Actualization.* TarcherPerigee, 2020.

Oliver, Mary. *Devotions: The Selected Poems of Mary Oliver.* Penguin Press, 2017.

Oliver, Mary. *Evidence: Poems.* Beacon Press, 2009.

Palmer, Parker J. *Let Your Life Speak: Listening for the Voice of Vocation.* Jossey-Bass, 1999.

Rohr, Richard. *Falling Upward: A Spirituality for the Two Halves of Life.* Jossey-Bass, 2011.

## Other Resources Worth Knowing About

Yurich, Ginny. 1000 Hours Outside: www.1000hoursoutside.com

National Park Service Junior Ranger Program: www.nps.gov/kids

Conner Prairie Interactive History Park: www.connerprairie.org

Red-tail Land Conservancy: www.redtaillandconservancy.org

*A Note on Sources:* Some of the science and research mentioned in this book comes from academic studies on forest medicine, attention restoration, interoceptive awareness, and the relationship between nature and well-being. If you're interested in the deep dive, start with the work of Rachel and Stephen Kaplan (attention restoration theory), Dr. Qing Li (forest medicine), and the growing body of research coming out of the Association of Nature & Forest Therapy.